SHE IS
UNSTOPPABLE™

vol. 1

Curated by Jennifer Hardie

She Is Unstoppable™

First edition: December 2018
Published in the United Kingdom

A CIP record of this book is available from The British Library

For information contact info@unstoppablebook.me

Cover design by **Sarah Shuttle**
Interior design by **Carole Chevalier**
Edits by **Jennifer Hardie, Sharon Woodcock & Authors**

Published with the support of **Team Author UK**.

For my family, the Unstoppable Community
and every woman out there with a dream...

*"May you always find the faith to remain strong through any storm,
whilst being a guiding light for others."*

Love always,
Jennifer Hardie

CONTENTS

Acknowledgements

A Note from the Curator

About Unstoppable

ACKNOWLEDGEMENTS

We would like to acknowledge the support, dedication and hard work of many wonderful people in the preparation of this book!

Including…

Our 12 magnificent authors! It has been an honour to bring your stories to fruition, thank you so much for being a part of this…Joanna Petrie-Rout, Cassandra Queeley, Robyn Chavarie, Bridget Zyka, Joyce Hardie, Natasha Leigh Bray, Cheryl White, Kate Bollanou, Rebecca Hawkes, Paulina Kapciak, Megan Frasier, Shannon Garrison Negi. You are all simply incredible!

Sharon Woodcock for your amazing storytelling, editing and proof-reading skills, you pored through each of these chapters with love and care. It has been a blessing to find and collaborate with you; I couldn't have done it with you.

Thank you also to the wonderful Fiona Hill who helped us by casting a talented eye over the stories too for the final checks, I appreciate you.

Sue Miller and her unbelievable team at Team Author UK, who appeared later on in the project as if by magic. Sue is the queen behind pulling it altogether, having the inside of the book designed along with the amazing designer, Carole Chevalier. Assisting with the self-publishing and printing along with David Casstles. You are simply irreplaceable, Sue. Here's to working on many more projects together!

So much appreciation for the talented Sarah Homan who designed the cover of our book. We asked for sleek, elegant yet strong and bold and you delivered in every way! Thank you.

To all of our mentors, coaches, teachers and our inspirations over the years who have said to us, 'you've got this' and motivated us to keep on moving forward, thank you! It is because of you all that we are brave enough to try new things each and every day, even when it scares us! Success is on the other side of fear, right!

Thank you to all of The Unstoppable Team too for helping me promote, organise and execute this project! You are all incredible.

A special shout out to Martina Ostradecky and Kumba Dauda who have been by my side from the very beginning, I appreciate all that you both do.

To all of our family and friends who are our rocks, our guiding lights, the glue that holds all of us together. We wouldn't be able to do any of this without each and every one of you by our side!

The Universe and all its magic. We all have unique beliefs, religions, rituals and spiritual paths so (to whatever that looks like for all of us) we want to give a huge divine thank you for blessing us all with the power to change the world. Change for the better! A little bit at a time.

We know you always have our back and we cannot wait to see how our paths unfold with your unshakeable belief and unwavering guidance.

Finally, You! Yes, you beautiful. Thank you again for picking this book up to read, we appreciate you so very much and cannot wait to see you in the secret society (see last page for details) real soon!

Finally, I would like to personally take the opportunity to thank my inspirations: my children – Joshua, Ruby & Joya. My husband Matt and my dog Bruce. You have always believed in me and even when times get tough and Mummy is working hard, you never fail to make me smile. Having you with me to remind me why I do all that I do is magical and I wouldn't be the woman I am without you. I love you all.

x

A NOTE FROM THE CURATOR

She Is Unstoppable™

First of all, I must give gratitude to you right now, in this moment! You could have chosen a million and one books to read but you are here with this one in your hand and for that I feel truly honoured! Thank you.

My hopes are that this book gives you inspiration and motivation. I hope it delivers a whole lot of laughs and moments of pensive thought and realisation too but most importantly, the complete unshakeable knowledge that you are never alone on this journey through life.

When the idea for this collaborative project presented itself to me that is how I felt. Alone and lost.

I was going through a time of low moods, anxiety and a sense of feeling unaligned to my business and furthermore, my life.

Around this time I was suffering from the pain of losing a dear friend and neighbour to cancer and also had another neighbour fighting cancer too. It was a time of great heartache.

All of this brought up old thoughts and feelings that I had experienced after the death of my cousin and best friend, Stewart, who took his own life at the age of 21. Feelings of confusion and uncertainty, feelings of hurt, anger and devastation.

I honestly felt that I had dealt with that pain and then out of nowhere it rises to the surface again and literally knocks you for six.

I am a strong woman, like you no doubt, and I tend to push my feelings to the side to be a pillar for others and push forward to support my family. I always felt so guilty letting my emotions show as 'how can I hurt the people I love by showing them how broken I feel' and 'I'm still here, I have this life to live and by feeling low like this, I'm taking it for granted'. However, at this time there was nothing else for it but to stop and take stock of these feelings and let them, quite literally, overflow.

I spent days in bed, meditating, praying, reading, crying and at one point…

A little voice whispered...

'You are not alone my love'.

What those simple words did for me in that moment was allowed me to really feel the emotions I was experiencing and not hold any guilt for it. It also removed the sense of loneliness. That trapped feeling of, 'no one else knows or understands what I am going through', so how can anyone help you?!

I knew exactly what I had to do. I had to speak up, I had to let go of my ego, my boundaries, this guard I had built and reach out to people.

I decided to reach out to some friends and tell them how I was feeling. Instantly they were sharing their own stories of times when they had felt exactly the same as I was describing.

I wasn't alone, nor had I ever been.

I'm here to tell you that someone, somewhere and no doubt very close by, has felt all that you have and are waiting to truly heal by helping support and heal you!

I remember thinking, 'If all of these strong, incredible women have felt this way, then there's no doubt many more women who haven't yet shared their stories with anyone.'

I reached out to my online community and asked...who would like to go on this journey with me? Who would like to write a book with me? Now, remember, this wasn't just sharing a story with a friend. I was asking them to share it with the world.

I couldn't believe it when over the space of a few days we had hundreds of women apply, so many brave, incredible women who were ready and willing to share a little of their soul with the world.

The next few months were intense as we selected our authors and began to put the wheels in motion. The raw chapters, the name for the book, the schedule, the team, the edits. So much to think about, such a huge amount of pressure and lots of dedication over the months to come but suddenly that sense of alignment came back to me.

This is what was missing!

See, my mission has always been to create platforms for women to showcase their successful businesses, their skills, their expertise, but never before had I created something for women, in which they could showcase and uncover just what it took to get there.

The women who feature in this book have all had to dig deep at many times in their lives, they have been strong but also felt weak. They have been resilient but at times given in. They have been lost and then relied on their heart to lead them to themselves again. They have felt lonely but never been alone.

And guess what... all of that needs to occur to help you step into the woman you were born to become.

I hope you find peace and reassurance that your pain can be turned into power.

Your crown doesn't slip when you show your true self to the world, in fact, it allows others to truly see the beauty of your soul.

Despite the darkness that at times ensues, there is always light; we have some hilarious stories in the book where the women share some of their younger years and 'hindsight' moments. It is also packed with inspiration and the most incredible global missions which I urge you to get involved with! (For a start, hint, hint, you can RSVP to your personal invite at the back of this book).

That's all from me, for now!

Kick back, relax and remember...

In order to become Unstoppable, we must at times stop!

Love always,

Jen x

P.S. Please do one little thing for us... once you've read this book could you pass it to a friend? Let's start a 'She Is Unstoppable' pay-it-forward chain to spread a little light and love into the world.

ABOUT UNSTOPPABLE

OUR MISSION...

Our mission is simple here at UNSTOPPABLE... to serve at the highest of standards and produce platforms for women to encompass all that they were born to be!

Over the past year we have created The Unstoppable Podcast Show – Unstoppable TV – Global Unstoppable Success Retreats – Business Academies – 1:1 services – self-study courses and this creative collaborative book writing project.

All of this is to support and showcase our ever-growing community of over 20k followers as they begin to design and bring into reality the life and business of their dreams.

UNSTOPPABLE women are driven, ambitious, heart-led, powerful and are catalysts for radical change in the world.

They nurture others, collaborate with fellow influencers, trust in their abilities and with quiet confidence carry themselves with an air of elegance and grace.

UNSTOPPABLE women practice and work on their credibility, ethics and integrity each and every day.

They are UNTOUCHABLE...

They are completely UNSTOPPABLE!

Jen Hardie
Award Winning Business Coach, Digital Marketing Strategist, Speaker, Writer, Author & Philanthropist

Robyn Chavarie

CHAPTER 1
Embracing All That I Am
By Robyn Chavarie

"The thing that is really hard, and really amazing, is giving up on being perfect and beginning the work of becoming yourself."
– Anna Quindlen

I had no idea what I was in for when I decided to embark on this journey of entrepreneurship.

In the online, service-based business world, we're taught to find our voice, own what makes us unique, and share our true and authentic selves with the world – but what if you're so disconnected that you don't even know who or what that is?

I see so many women suffering, not living their purpose, not giving themselves permission to even think about their dreams or say them out loud, let alone live them.

I was one of those women.

When I started my business, I was blind to how my perfectionist and people-pleasing ways were sabotaging me. I had put up so many layers of protection over the years that I didn't even know how to be myself anymore. I thought I could push, force, hustle and work my way to success, controlling everything from my masculine energy.

I had a very wholesome childhood growing up in New Brunswick, Canada. I spent most of my time in nature and with my family, learning how to fish and hunt and to explore my surroundings. I remember how my mom would dress me up in frilly dresses with pantyhose for school and I'd come home bleeding, knees ripped out of them from playing on the playground. I was also incredibly creative and artistic, and I'd spend hours in my room by myself with a book or drawing and coloring.

I'm highly introverted with a sprinkle of spunk and sass, and I'm stubborn as a bull. I've always been one to question the rules and make my own, and heaven forbid if I didn't get my own way. (It's so clear to me now that I was destined for the entrepreneurial path.)

At the same time, I have always been highly sensitive, and I remember frequently being overwhelmed with emotion as a child. I didn't know how to deal with it or process. I remember crying a lot when having to say goodbye to relatives, or during movies, even at the happy endings! My Grampy calls it being 'tender-hearted'.

My parents were strict with me and I always strived to be the good girl, but the duality of wanting to do it my way and learn my own lessons while at the same time wanting to please my parents, family, and those around me, made me feel suffocated and always under pressure.

For following my parents' rules, being a good student in school, always striving to achieve more and be the best, I was always rewarded greatly.

I wanted to please everyone...

My great-grandmother, who was like a mother to me and the epitome of unconditional love, who used to carry me around when I was a baby like I was hers. We had a very special relationship.

My dad, who traveled a lot for work and who I missed dearly when he was gone.

My teachers, so I could get the praise and high grades and feel accomplished.

My peers at school, who bullied me. I never fitted in.

I didn't know my worth wasn't found in a boy's crush, a gold star from my teacher, how many friends I had, or an, 'I'm proud of you', from family.

I looked everywhere for validation that I was enough, except within myself. This is how we are programmed – be better than everyone else, life is a competition, you have to fit in to be liked and loved, it's all about the score – these are the ways you find happiness.

Especially as women, we are fed this message from a young age. No one tells us we can thrive by just being ourselves, or from the power and intuition we possess as women. We are taught to conform to society's rules, to measure our worth by the way we look, and our intelligence, and our ability to perform.

I learned to disconnect from my intuition, my own desires, and quiet my inner voice. It seemed so much easier to do that than to go against the grain and cause trouble. As a teenager, the disconnection from myself only worsened.

I developed early as a young woman, and my teens were an especially difficult few years with raging hormones and trying to figure out who I was in this world.

When my parents found out about my first sexual experience, I was left feeling vulnerable and ashamed. No one wants to talk about sex with their parents, but for me, it went so much deeper. I had always wanted to please my parents, my family, and be the good girl they knew me to be, but instead, I was left feeling like my sexuality was something to be ashamed about.

I continued to disconnect from my inner Goddess and put up walls of protection.

A few years later, I was the victim of sexual assault by another student in my high school. I remember feeling like it was my fault, as though I had done something to deserve it or bring on that behavior. I was called all kinds of names. I had friends ask me not to report it, to not get the guy in trouble and ruin his life and future career. More conversations about sex with my parents and the authorities left me wanting to crawl out of my own skin.

Of course, I shut off my connection to my body and to my power. The only messages I was hearing from my family, at school, church, in the media – overwhelmingly – was that my feminine power, my body, and my sexual energy, the way I was created as a woman, was something to be ashamed of and that should be hidden.

I felt like I had to hide that side of me to be loved and accepted. It was how I protected myself. I was incredible at putting up walls and pretending that everything was ok, while inside I continued to stifle the chaos. I was a highly sensitive person in a world where being that way didn't get you ahead.

Being in my masculine is what got me praise, and made me feel accomplished. It's what helped me to control what happened in my life, whereas, being open and vulnerable in my feminine was overwhelming and painful. So, I learned to shut it down, turn it off, and disconnect from my body.

Our feminine energy is what magnetizes us to our ideal clients, our soulmates, our tribe. It's what allows us to create and birth our work into the world. It brings play, pleasure, joy, and contentment into our daily lives.

What do you think happens when you start to believe...

You're too sensitive.

You're too sexual.

You're too much.

The way you were created by the Universe is shameful.

You are not enough as you are.

You have to hide to be accepted.

And you're supposed to show up online, and be visible and vulnerable to connect with people?

Well, it's scary as hell, and it takes a lot of courageous internal work to break through.

I've always been a high achiever – taking all advanced courses in high school, competing in the Canada Games for Biathlon, working as many hours as I could squeeze in – so when I went out on my own just after high school, I turned up the volume on my hustle and worked full-time during my first year of university. I went from working in kitchens to getting my first call center job with over a $1 an hour increase (I was making bank!), and it was there that I met my husband.

He was so outgoing and wasn't afraid to speak his mind. I fell head-over-heels. I saw a whole new world with him and broke out of my sheltered, structured shell. We moved in together almost immediately and from then on have been virtually inseparable.

A few years after we met, we had an incredible opportunity to move to Florida for work. We had no savings, and barely a plan, but we quit our jobs, stuffed whatever we could into our car, including our traveling cats, and moved what felt like a million miles away from home.

It was difficult being away from family and everything I knew growing up, and I threw myself into my career, feeling like I had something to prove – not only to others but to myself — that I could make it on my own. I was an independent woman, dammit! As a perfectionist, I didn't take criticism well, but I could make things happen, and I pushed myself to do things faster and better than everyone else.

Fast forward ten years and I had the life most would dream about. An incredible husband, and a new home we could call our own. I was at the top of my career, financially stable, and in the best shape I had been in years – but inside I was yearning for more.

In all that time I had never stopped to ask myself what I really wanted from life. I was excellent at becoming a chameleon and fitting in with whoever I was surrounded by at the time, but I never allowed myself to think about if what I had was enough.

My inner Goddess was awakening.

I was grateful for everything I had and the life I had built, but deep down I never felt like I was able to be myself. I knew I wouldn't spend the next forty years doing the same routine day in and day out. I put a lot of pressure on myself to be the best and suffered from tension headaches and severe anxiety.

If I can just be perfect and control everything, including others' opinions of me, everything will be fine!

(Starting to get the picture of how finding your purpose and following your soul's calling isn't as simple as filling out a branding worksheet and picking out a business name?)

I knew there was more out there for me. I knew I wanted something that turned me back on to life and lit up my soul. I knew I had more to offer and I just wanted to help people dream bigger for themselves and get out of victim mode.

But because I had silenced that inner guidance system so many years before, I had no clear vision of what I truly wanted for myself, or what would bring me that fulfilment and happiness. When I started my own online business, I carried those patterns and limiting beliefs with me.

I didn't know how to show up as my true self. I was supposed to be connecting with people online, building relationships, but I had spent so many years hiding my real self as a form of protection that I didn't know who Robyn really was anymore. My surface level personal development and motivation techniques weren't doing anything to get to the root of my suffering and disconnection.

I was still people-pleasing and trying to be perfect. I was still carrying that deep-seated belief that I wasn't enough and it would be shameful to let someone see the real me.

You can't fully open up and serve your clients if you aren't willing to heal those wounds.

The masculine energy I had been living in for so long took over, and I threw myself into my business. I got promoted really quickly and was given all kinds of great attention from my mentors. It drove me to push harder, but even with my success, I wasn't feeling the fulfillment I thought my business would bring me. I was showing up in ways that were unaligned with who I am, pushing for that next promotion, copying what all the leaders were doing and teaching, instead of focusing on helping people.

I thought that's what I had to do to be successful. I never stopped to ask myself if I was actually enjoying the process and if what I was creating felt aligned with me.

I eventually burned out...

I had gained 40 plus pounds (even while a part of a health and wellness company), spent two years ignoring my husband with my nose in my phone every spare moment, checking out completely at work to the point of almost getting fired (twice) and transformed into someone I could no longer recognize.

I was stuck in unbalanced, masculine energy, and I had forgotten how to enjoy life. I was all force, drive, hustle, and it wasn't even on my radar to slow down and 'surrender'.

I knew I needed guidance and it came in the form of a life coach.

One of my business mentors had mentioned she was working with someone on one of her trainings, and I remember thinking, 'maybe that's what I need!'. A few weeks later I had the thought to reach out to my mentor to get the coach's information, and that very day, she walked into the gym during my workout. I had never seen this woman in public outside of a planned event in over two years, even though she lived in my same small town.

Ok Universe, I get the friggin' message!

My soul was speaking to me, and I was finally ready to listen.

Working with multiple coaches, and traveling all over the world for retreats over the last few years, has taken me down a path of self-awareness like I never could have imagined.

When you open yourself up to being called out on your own B.S. with love and respect, your life changes.

I was TERRIFIED to be seen for who I truly am.

That fear kept me hidden for years in my business and in my relationships.

I know now how to get out of my head, back into my body and back into the present.

To get relief from the constant anxiety and overwhelm by remembering that I am genuinely whole, exactly as I am.

I am a perfectly imperfect human.

I am stardust and love and light.

My tears are not something to be ashamed of or that I needed to try and hide, they are simply one of the ways I process emotion.

I am not my past.

My feminine and sexual energy are where my POWER comes from.

I had snuffed out all my creativity and magnetism because I had closed off the connection to my most powerful gift. (Can I say VAGINA POWER! In here?)

I had forgotten my worthiness didn't come from others' validation or my own outward accomplishments. I started to see myself in the eyes of my great-grandmother, guardian angel.

I started to recognize my own innate gifts for holding space for other transformations.

And that's when a fire was lit inside of me so powerful it cannot be extinguished.

Working with a coach, it became so clear to me that I was supposed to be helping women in this way, and that I had been doing it my entire life. I was always the listener, the one that people came to for advice.

Turning that into a business when I had come from the employee world where everything was done for me, to now figuring it all out from scratch – well, that was a journey in and of itself.

I started a group program with three women and launched my idea. I was obsessed with the work immediately. Watching women overcome mindset struggles keeping them stuck, that they had held on to for years, was like someone filling me up with love and light.

For the next year, I dabbled, trying to figure out how to turn that into a business. I finally had to have a talk with myself. If I was going to turn this into a real business and do it for the rest of my life, I was going to have to take it seriously and start treating it that way.

I hired a business coach and learned how to turn my innate gifts into a profitable business that I love. I've traveled to Costa Rica and Bali and met some of the most phenomenal women in the industry. I don't do it for the money, I do it for the impact and the fulfillment it brings me. I'm transforming lives and awakening women to their power. I'm determined to save women years of pain and frustration in their business by helping them with what they are missing, the first, most crucial piece: CLARITY.

One of my most incredible clients came to me feeling stuck in every area of her life. She was unhappy with her living situation, frustrated at work, and unhappy in her own skin because she had gained weight after her divorce from a narcissistic ex-husband. She felt like her life wasn't going anywhere and didn't know the next step to take. She had so much emotion bottled up inside of her and no outlet to process it.

My gifts are to help women realize that it's not about escaping your current life, it's about remembering who you are, getting crystal clear about what it is that you want, and giving yourself permission to have it. When you can heal those subconscious beliefs, you can change your entire life.

We are not our past. This client was finally about to see her worthiness wasn't determined by her ex-husband's harsh words, the bullying she experienced as a young girl, or her weight and how she felt in her body. She was able to step back into her power and be happy and confident in her own skin.

She gave herself permission to be the woman she truly wanted to be, letting go of the expectations of her family and friends, and found herself again. She was able to release so much of the anxiety and need to control everything and surrender to her desires. She uncovered her purpose to help other women feel confident again and has started her own online business doing just that. She is doing work that lights her up and is no longer afraid to be seen and go after what she really wants in life.

She was even thankful for her divorce and other experiences because she knew they got her to where she is today. How many people can say that?

You might ask why I put myself through all of that growth and chaos. Opening those old wounds and doing the shadow work is far from a comfortable experience. I had the life most people yearn for.

I do it for women like that one client. I did it because there was no other option. I did it because I was finally ready to start listening to my soul. Once you begin to hear your calling, no amount of pushing it away or trying to silence it will make it go away or be quiet.

My mission is to help women entrepreneurs find their purpose, step back into their power, and own their unique gifts so they can make the impact they desire, and create the business and life of their dreams.

You get to create a business that's an extension of you, to show up as your true self, to do the work that lights you up, and you get paid really well to do it.

And if you don't believe me, let me lend you my belief until you have your own.

Xoxo
Robyn

Final Words of Wisdom:

1. Find yourself first. Before you go searching for happiness outside of you, remember who you are at your core, that will always lead you home. Your intuition is your most powerful tool if you learn to listen.

2. Seek Clarity before strategy. Know what you want. Know what lights you up and what you don't like doing. When you know who you are, how you want to show up, and where you're going, it's so simple to make decisions about your day-to-day life and your business.

3. Give yourself permission. No one out there is going to do it for you. Let go of the expectations of others and give yourself permission to dream bigger.

4. Lose the labels. I'm an introverted Gemini, INFJ, Empath, yoga student, world traveler, recovered nail biter, etc. But I don't let a label define me or use it as an excuse to stay where I am. There are literally no rules.

5. Stop searching for fearlessness. The fear comes when we are getting out of our comfort zone and rising to our next level. Start looking at the fear as excitement until both energies feel the same in your body.

ABOUT THE AUTHOR

Robyn Chavarie is a Business and Clarity Coach for heart-centered women entrepreneurs who want to use their unique gifts to create a business and life by their own design.

Robyn spent most of her twenties hustling for the big life goals – getting ahead in her career, buying a house, getting married, saving money for retirement – checking all the boxes that are supposed to make you feel successful and accomplished. And although she felt pride and gratitude for her life, she knew she wanted more. She was craving fulfilment in her work and the permission to be herself.

Shortly after her thirtieth birthday, her awakening (or as she likes to call it – third life crisis) began. She started struggling with her weight, not feeling good enough, and hearing that deep inner calling that life was meant to be joyful, not full of pressure and anxiety. She was already seeing success building her 'side hustle' on top of her full-time job, but that was also beginning to feel out of alignment.

Showing up the way others were teaching her to build an online business was just creating more of that overwhelming pressure. She now clearly sees that it was precisely what she needed to propel her into the work she does today – helping other women get back in touch with themselves so they can create a business they love.

Her mission now is to help other women start their business from a place of clarity and total alignment. She is a badass Goddess that uses energetic healing, mindset work, and customized strategy that helps you step back into your power and unleash your highest self.

ROBYN CHAVARIE

Business and Clarity Coach for heart-centered women.
www.robynchavarie.com

- f @robynchavarie
- f @mycoachrobyn (business)
- @robynchavarie

Cheryl White

CHAPTER 2
Surviving to Thriving
By Cheryl White

"You always had the power my dear, you just had to learn it for yourself."
– The Wizard of Oz

I grew up in Birkenhead, on Merseyside, as the oldest of four children. I have two brothers, Daniel and Steven, and my sister, Gemma. We grew up in a very working-class family, surrounded by our mum and dad, aunties, uncles, and grandparents. I had a really lovely childhood filled with love and laughter. When I was little, and at school, I made lots of friends, and they're still my friends now. That's the kind of place I grew up in... community was everything and people would go out of their way to show that. We didn't have much money. My mum and dad did the best they could, but as they had four kids, it was difficult for them at times. Money can't buy happiness though, and we had happiness by the bucket load!

I loved school from the age of four. My mum dropped me off for an hour of 'settling in' to see how I got on, and I ended up staying for the whole day because I loved it so much. I enjoyed being around people. Secondary school was good too. I was pretty popular and had lots of friends. I was also a bit of a teacher's pet. I worked really hard and did very well in my exams. I was involved in the dance and drama side of school and loved singing, and I still love singing now! I also studied English and History. They were my favourite subjects. English Literature started my passion for reading. I enjoy reading, and I still love to read whenever I get the opportunity.

I remember when I was fourteen, my parents split up and the four of us lived with my dad, which was quite a difficult time because my dad had to go out and work. Mum was still very much around, but she didn't live with us anymore. I quickly took on the role of 'mum' and looked after the others, given I was the eldest, and my dad worked most of the time.

Back then, I resented it because I didn't have the same freedom as my friends. I always had to be home to make sure the children got in from school and then cook the tea and do other household things. When I look back on that period, I think it made me the person I am now because I'm very organised and independent. It's actually done me more good than harm.

At the time though, I just wanted to go out with my friends and do the usual things teenagers do. I was quite held back by that. Although things were often difficult, there was also still lots of love and laughter. My brothers have always made me laugh with the things they do and say. We were always playing tricks on my dad, and my brothers would often put books above an open door so they fell on my dad when he walked in the room, or we'd hide in the cupboard under the stairs and scare him when he opened it. There are so many stories I can think of, and when the four of us are together now we laugh at all the mischief we got up to.

After secondary school, I had a bit of a wobble. I went to the local Sixth Form College and enrolled to do A-Levels. I took English, History, and Sociology. About twelve months into doing my A-Levels, I decided I'd had enough of them. I wanted to get a job and work. I never had any money. Everybody was always going out and I couldn't. All of my friends had left school and got jobs. I was the only one who had gone on to secondary education.

Much to my dad's disgust, I left college after twelve months and gave up my A-Levels. I worked as a dental nurse at a local dentist's, and that's when I realised that I actually loved looking after and caring for people. I did dental nursing for about seven or eight months and then enrolled in university to do my degree in nursing. I went back to night school and finished my A-Levels which I had to do before I could get into university.

I loved spending time with my friends back then. We discovered alcohol, and used to try to get into pubs we weren't supposed to go into. One day, I was sat in a pub drinking cider with my friends, and my dad and his friend walked in! I spent the next three hours sat under the table in case he saw me, with my friends passing drinks to me, so I didn't feel left out!

I've always had a passion for horses, and every weekend I'd be at the stables helping out and riding. I think I got paid something like thirty pounds a week and that, to me, was a massive amount of money. It gave me the freedom I wanted to go and do my own thing. I used the money to pay for driving lessons and passed my driving test at the age of seventeen. I was finally independent!

When I was eighteen, I went on to do my nursing degree, which was really hard. I didn't quite realise just how difficult it would be. I was doing forty hours a week on the wards in Liverpool and studying at the same time for three full years. I absolutely loved nursing, and all the patients and people I met. It was just the studying side I struggled with sometimes. Not academically, I just didn't want to do it as I felt my time would be spent better on the wards, learning from other nurses. But I did do it, and after three years I passed my degree and became a fully qualified adult nurse. During that time, I actually bought my first house too, which was a massive achievement.

I'd always wanted to be a community nurse and look after patients in their own homes, but I needed twelve-months' experience first. I became a community nurse on the Wirral, which is where I live, and I quickly got promoted to a senior nurse within twelve months. This made me feel really proud of everything I had achieved as I was one of the youngest senior nurses on the Wirral team. I worked in this role for the next fifteen years.

The high point of my job was definitely the difference I made to people's lives. Not just to my patients' lives, but to their family members as well. I would go to see patients, and sometimes it would just be leg wounds or dressings, or catheter care, but a lot of my work was palliative care. I nursed people who were dying. I made people comfortable in their own homes and supported their family members. I still see a lot of the patients' families now, whose family members have passed away up to twenty years ago, and they still come up to me and say, 'I remember how you looked after my mum or my dad, I will always be grateful to you'. It's a lovely feeling to know you made such a difficult time for somebody that little bit easier.

I'd say the low points in nursing were the really long hours. A lot of the nurses were very stressed with some of the situations we had to deal with. Sometimes we had safeguarding issues, and a lot of our patients were elderly. Sometimes, I've heartbreakingly gone into a patient's home, and the elderly person I've been looking after has confided in me that they were either being abused emotionally by their family members, or physically abused. I've actually had reports of sexual abuse from elderly relatives as well. They were the low points; it's difficult to deal with that and to leave it at the door when you come home.

I remember one of my clients so vividly. She had been diagnosed with lung cancer, and I went in to see her after my maternity leave. She was completely flat. She'd been given hours to live, and I found it really unusual with her being so young that she had deteriorated so quickly. When I looked through her notes, I noticed she had been a heroin addict and that there was no substitute of heroin in her syringe driver. So, I contacted the nurses who were caring for her, and they prescribed a substitute. We put it in, and within twelve hours she was sat up in bed, talking to her family, eating Indian food from the local Indian takeaway. That lady will always stick in my mind. She was such a character, in fact, her whole family were such characters. She was amazing and I'll always remember how quickly she'd come round when I visited. She used to say, 'Oh, where's my angel? She brought me back'. And we would have a little laugh about it. She then went on to live for another eighteen months before she died of cancer. I know I made such a massive difference to her and her family, and that makes me feel proud of the nurse I was.

On the other end of the scale, there was a lady I'll always remember. She was thirty-four, and she had cancer. She was a pharmacist at the local hospital so she knew all the drugs we were giving her in the syringe driver which often made her very distressed. I visited her one day, and her two children, who were only about three and seven were sat on the sofa in the living room. It was at half-past eight in the morning, and they were eating crisps for their breakfast. I said, 'Where's your mum?' And they told me she was upstairs in bed and had not got up that morning. I walked up the stairs calling her, and when I got to the side of her bed, I realised she had passed away. The children had been downstairs on their own.

Moments like this are utterly devastating, but you go into auto-pilot in those situations. It's what you're trained to do, and when you come away from it, you've got your team there to support you. I had a great team of nurses, and we'd talk about what had happened and support each other. Sometimes it would get too much, and we'd put somebody on lesser duties to give them some time and space.

I don't think you ever forget the sad times. You never leave it at the door.

I think overall that I managed it quite well, really. I'm a very strong and independent person and you kind of deal with things as they come up. It takes an awful lot to upset me or to really get to me. You've got to detach yourself from it as much as you can. When I speak to other nurses, their coping mechanisms tend to be the same. You have to think, what can we do to support the people that are left or to support other members of the team. I did deal with it really well until we started to get more and more added to our workload.

When I started nursing, I used to have four patients a day. I was able to deal with that amount and had lots of time to spend with them, time to process what needed to be done and how I could do more for them.

When I left the nursing in 2014, I was sometimes going to visit fifteen patients a day. I thought it was so dangerous and saw the stress levels of the staff start to creep up. I saw many of our staff leave or go off on long-term sick. It was awful because we were told we could now only spend fifteen minutes per patient. If you have somebody who needs to speak to you about something or is in pain, you can't say to the patient, 'well, I'm sorry, I've got to leave now. I've only got 15 minutes with you'. Most of the time I was supposed to finish work at five, but I was often still there at seven o'clock at night because we had all the paperwork side of it to do as well.

My beautiful boy Daniel came when I was thirty and then William when I was thirty-seven.

I had been nursing for over ten years by that point, and when Dan came along, my outlook on life changed. I didn't want to be having to work until seven o'clock at night. I wanted to be a mum that was there to pick him up, that could go to all the school plays, that could go on the school trips and I just didn't have that flexibility as a nurse.

I started to look at other ways I could earn money. That's when I thought about the social care service where I live, which runs in parallel with the nursing service. The service up until this point, however, was dreadful. For years I had struggled to find good care providers to complement our nursing service. So, I decided I was going to set up Apollo Care.

I got the idea when I was on maternity leave back in 2008. The first thing I knew I needed to do was to write some policies and procedures to become the backbone for the business. I started to write them, and I ended up writing fifty-something of them because there were that many I felt I needed to do. I then decided I wanted to write all of my own assessment documentation for hiring staff too. I wanted to do all of it myself because with my nursing background I knew they'd be perfect.

I am a control freak, can you tell?!

I just wanted everything to be how I wanted it to be. I thought it would have taken a few months, but it actually took me three years to set up the business, write all of the paperwork and get it all just how I wanted it. I still worked as a nurse for four days a week while I was setting up the business. Finally, I was ready to launch it in 2011.

In the beginning, I'm not going to lie, things were tough. I had to work eight until five every day, sometimes until seven or eight o'clock at night. I'd come home, sort the baby out, put him in bed and then I'd be sat up until two, three o'clock in the morning writing policies and procedures for the new business. At the time, it felt a million miles away. I used to think 'why am I doing this?'. My partner Mark and I would often fall out, he said, 'All you're doing is writing and on the computer. I never see you anymore', but I just knew I had to do something. I needed to get out of the NHS, and for me, that was the way forward.

Mark has always been very supportive of me despite his understandable frustration, for not spending as much time with him as he'd liked. He was worried about me because I was so stressed and working all the time. I was exhausted. We couldn't go out for a meal without the on-call phone ringing. I questioned whether I was doing the right thing. I thought, 'if I give all this up now, I could go back to having an easy life'. I was getting a good wage for nursing. I had so many doubts in the back of my mind. I also had family members saying, 'Why are you going to leave a good job? You've worked so hard to become a nurse'. In the end, I think I just became resilient to all of that and started to look at my long-term plan.

It was Dan who kept me going. I don't think I'd have ever started my business if it hadn't been for him. I was happy to plod along and earn the same amount of money each month and live in the same house.

As soon as I saw the baby, I knew I had to give him more. Not in a materialistic sense, it was more in terms of time. I could foresee what was going to happen, I'd be dropping him off at school at eight o'clock, picking him up at six o'clock and then he'd be in bed for half six, and I just thought, 'I don't want that to happen. I want to spend as much time as I can with him, and I want to always be around when he comes home from school'. I started to think that the minute he was born.

That's where the sheer determination came from; by this point, I'd just had enough of nursing and the organisation I worked for. I figured 'if I don't do something about it, this is where I'm going to be stuck for the next thirty or forty years'. I'd seen other nurses in exactly the same position, and I didn't want that to happen to me.

When it came to my new business, I don't want to tell you it was easy... there were times I sat and cried and thought, why am I doing this? I've had enough of it. I had no business background whatsoever and was sort of fumbling my way along. I found that every time I overcame something, another obstacle would come up straight after. I wanted a better life for Dan, but I also wanted a better life for me. I knew I couldn't earn any more than what I was making as a nurse. I'd reached the top of the pay scale, and I thought if I want to go on nice holidays, if I want to get a bigger house, I'm going to have to do something about it. It's only me that can do it. My uncle always worked for himself, and I remember him saying to me, 'You'll never ever earn enough money while you're working for somebody else, you've got to work for yourself'. I must have only been about eleven, but it always stuck in my mind, That's when I started thinking, 'if I set up a business one day it would give me a better life', but it took until Dan was born to make it happen.

So, my business launched in 2011, and thankfully my mum had just taken early retirement, so she came in to help me to manage it. We were actually working from my mum's living room with a mobile phone. That's all we had. We had a couple of staff waiting to start with us once we got some care packages in place, and I stupidly thought that once we told a couple of people we had begun, the calls would start coming in. That was in April, and we waited and waited, and finally, we got our first call in July.

It was a painfully slow start for us to get going, but when I look back now, I didn't do any launch, I didn't create any marketing material, I didn't do anything. I just waited for people to hear about us, and then wondered why it wasn't happening!

The very first phone call we got, was when we were at my mum's house. The phone rang, and I shouted, 'You pick it up', and she said, 'no, you pick it up'! When we finally answered, it was the wrong number! We were both disappointed and knew we had to change how we were doing things. We started to go out and speak to voluntary organisations and social workers. My mum literally drove around the Wirral and talked to lots of different agencies to find us work. We finally got our first couple of clients through word of mouth, and I'm delighted to say that the momentum built up from there.

I told my mum I still wanted to nurse a couple of days a week. I wanted the care agency to have no more than thirty clients, and to keep it as a really small agency. Within the first eight months, we had over thirty clients, and we continued to grow and grow. I was still nursing, looking after Dan, and running the business. I ended up in hospital, because I thought I was having a heart attack, but it was actually stress palpitations.

I was so stressed trying to run everything, and at one point, I had four mobile phones in my pocket. One was my own, one was for the Apollo business, one was the on-call nursing phone, and one was the out-of-hours phone. At one point, three of them started ringing together, and I knew then that I couldn't carry on this way.

I had to choose between the business and nursing. I decided to give up nursing which was really upsetting, because even though I was very overworked, I loved the team I worked with. After I gave up nursing, within three months of me working full-time on the business, we doubled in size. Business was thriving because I was now giving it my full attention. We were getting calls from all over Merseyside. Family members were starting to hear about us. People got really distressed when we told them we had no availability. I just didn't know what to do with the business. It was growing and growing.

After eighteen months of trading I was working sixty-hours a week on the business. I hardly saw baby Dan. I had a full office team and thirty-eight care staff, but I just felt like I'd taken five steps forward and ten steps back. I had a business that was generating lots of money, but I didn't have time to breathe. I realised I had to do something about it, so I spoke to my accountant, and we decided to franchise the business.

When my accountant first suggested franchising, I said, 'It sounds like a really good idea', and then went and googled 'What is franchising?' in the car because I had no idea what she meant and didn't want to look stupid! But after looking into it, I thought it would be perfect for me, and the ideal business model I needed to create. I researched franchise consultants and found a local one who wasn't as expensive as the others. It was very, very expensive to franchise, so, I went to her for advice. I borrowed the money from my mum, and I started my franchise journey.

At this point, I found out that I was expecting my second baby, William. Although very excited, I was also worried. I had started my business to give Dan a better life, yet I was working all the time and constantly felt guilty. How would I find more time to give to another baby? I was full of hope that adopting the franchise model would help me to gain some of my time back and be the mum I wanted to be. I now had two little people to think of and I knew I had to make this work. It really was make or break now!

However, the franchise consultant really let me down. The paperwork she produced was shoddy, and had lots of spelling mistakes, and the name of another business dotted here and there; she'd obviously cut and pasted sections from paperwork she'd prepared for another company. It was a disaster and the legal document was awful. I had a terrible time with the franchising process, and at the end of it, I didn't understand what I was supposed to be doing. I felt overwhelmed and under-supported. I had two choices, give up or improve things...

I rewrote all of the documents she had sent me and made them relevant to my business. I then hired the best solicitors in Liverpool to produce a water-tight legal document to protect my business moving forward. I spent hours reading about the franchise process, determined to learn everything I could. I'm glad I didn't give up as I sold two franchises in the first couple of months to two of my senior care staff and I then sold the original business I'd set up, Apollo Care, as a franchise.

I then had three franchises operating under the Apollo name, and I turned over just under £200,000 in my first year of franchising. My life was starting to change because of the franchise model I had formed within my business.

Once I had sold the main care agency as a franchise, straight away I had an injection of money to put into the business, which took away my financial stress. I paid off my mortgage, invested some of the money, and bought myself a new car. I also treated my family, which was lovely to be able to do after working so hard.

My stress literally disappeared overnight.

Because I wasn't running the central care agencies anymore, I dropped from working a sixty-hour week to a fifteen-hour a week. My role became supporting the franchise teams instead of running the day-to-day care agency. I suddenly felt back in control and able to manage what I had created.

My next step was to start looking where else I could sell the franchises. I started with the Liverpool area, and we quickly sold all five areas in Liverpool within the first couple of years. Our company reputation was growing, and people wanted to be a part of it. The fourth franchise I sold was to a fellow who came to do some training with my Wirral teams. He did some training with my franchisees on dementia and was so impressed with the business and the ethos behind the business that he and his daughter bought our fourth franchise.

When I look at where the business was five years ago, when I first franchised, to where it is now, it's just unrecognisable. I've got all of the systems and strategies in place that I didn't have back then. I've got a head office team who run the business for me, which allows me to dip in and out of the business.

Apollo Care keeps growing and growing. The branding is becoming huge around our local Merseyside area. Collectively, the Apollo Care brand turns over £250,000 each month now compared to five years ago when it was turning over just under £18,000 a month. So, you can see how quickly the business has scaled through franchising, but the most important thing is, my stress levels are fine. I don't worry about my business, because now I'm collaborating and have a team there to pass that work over to, which is absolutely essential.

Over time, I started to get more interested in how to franchise, and what documents you need and what they should look like. That's how Mercury Franchise School, my other business came about. It was a natural progression because I'd had to rewrite everything myself when the franchise consultant didn't do a great job.

One day, a local business woman came into my office. She asked me about the franchise process and how it had changed my business, so I told her my story. After a long chat she asked me if I would consider helping her to franchise her business. I was a bit taken aback! I thought it through and decided that I could help her. We agreed on a price, and I helped her write all of the documents, and explained the process as we went along. She franchised her business with me and sold her first franchise after a couple of weeks. I then realised it was a niche in the market that was needed. So, I set up Mercury Franchise Consultancy at the end of 2015, where people came to me, and I franchised their business for them.

After the business had been trading for twelve months, I knew I needed to change things. I felt uncomfortable about the way the business operated. I was franchising people's businesses for them, but I wanted to empower business owners to learn the process for themselves, just as I did, with my support and knowledge. I then changed the business to Mercury Franchise School which teaches people how to franchise their business themselves.

During the process, we go through all the documentation, and how franchising works. We give sample documentation, and marketing advice through a ten-month online, one to one, course. At the end of that ten-month period, that business owner has got a franchise business. We've been doing that now for about twelve months, and it's worked exceptionally well. We help people to sell a franchise before they've actually finished the process with us, so they get their investment back. Business owners complete the course with all the documents and knowledge they need to grow their business using the franchise model.

We also support franchisors who have already franchised their business, and are feeling a little stuck with their marketing and systems and need some help with a re-model and fresh ideas. This is done on a one-to-one basis and in regular workshops.

The big vision for me is to build up both businesses and my teams to support me with the day-to-day running. I totally believe that if you have the right people in place, you can support them and teach them how to do anything. I've already got a franchise support manager in place now for Apollo Care and my plan for her in the next twelve months is to train her to become my business manager. My Apollo head office team consists of four people which I plan to expand to six over the next twelve months. Delegation is key to growing a successful business that can run without you.

I am also building the Mercury team. My franchise coaches have got to be franchisors. They need to know the franchising process and actually be living it as they are now. Experience teaches us all so much and my coaches will be able to pass that experience on to others, helping them to grow a franchise model and create a franchise team.

The main tip I would give to a business owner who's trying to build their business is to take action every single day, even if you get up and you're tired, stressed, and overworked. It's just doing one thing each day to move that dream forward. Have the main goal within your vision of where you want to be and create steps every single day to get you there. Never compare your day one to somebody else's day twenty. If you're making progress, it doesn't matter how slow it is as long as you get to your end goal.

Self-development is also a key factor to any success! I started practicing self-development about two years ago. I was so business-focused that I didn't really take any notice of me and what I wanted, and needed to be a great leader and to inspire others. Now, it's all about self-development for me, and I do lots of reading. At the moment, I'm really interested in Reiki, chakras and how energy affects us all. I'm starting to learn more about that and how I can bring it into my coaching to help my clients.

CHERYL WHITE

Franchise strategist and franchisor.

- @MercuryFranchiseSchool
- @buildafranchiseempire (group)
- @cherylwhitefranchising

ABOUT THE AUTHOR

Franchise strategist and franchisor, Cheryl is an advocate for female entrepreneurs who want to have it all. She is the founder of the online Mercury Franchise School and Apollo Care Franchising Limited and has made it her mission to help as many business owners as possible create a franchise empire from the business they love, without sacrificing their time.

Franchising her own business in 2013, Cheryl realised the power that the franchise model had to not only create a business empire but also to produce the ultimate passive income, giving her the much-wanted time to spend with her family and creating her dream lifestyle.

Franchise consultancy methods concerned Cheryl and she felt that women were not given the support, encouragement and empowerment they deserved by the 'do it for you' method.

She knew that she needed to change things and created a ripple of unease in the franchise industry when she created her first DIY franchise course in 2015. She wanted to teach female business owners how to franchise their business themselves, support them through the process and provide them with sample documentation to show them how to produce their own beautiful, informative documents that made their business shine.

Franchising her own business was the turning point when turnover went up from £100,000 per year to almost £1,000,000 after just 4 years of trading. She knew she needed to teach this method to as many business owners as she could.

Since launching Mercury Franchise School, Cheryl has helped her clients to grow their businesses, create a passive income and get their time back.

Her signature system empowers women to take control of their lives, develop new methods of working and completely shift their mindset to what is possible. Cheryl is proof that her methods work and now wants to share these methods with you!

When not building empires, Cheryl can be found spending time with her 2 beautiful sons, riding her horse or walking her dogs.

"The meaning of life is to find your gift, the purpose of life is to give it away."

– Pablo Picasso

Rebecca Hawkes

CHAPTER 3
You Can Achieve Anything You Put Your Mind To
By Rebecca Hawkes

"It does not do well to dwell on dreams and forget to live."
– Albus Dumbledore

My life has been full of transformations. Some have taken months, others a matter of weeks. The biggest one, and the catalyst for my future transformations happened a few months before my twenty-first birthday...

Between the ages of eighteen and twenty, I became unexplainably very anxious. If someone spoke to me, my heart would race, my palms would get clammy, and I'd forget how to talk. I'd laugh nervously as the voice in my head would tell me how rude I was being and how everyone was judging me for being weird. When I look back now, I know it was anxiety. At the time though, I just thought something was wrong with me.

Before the anxiety hit, I'd started a new job and was full of confidence, excitement and willingness to learn as much as I could so I could climb the career ladder. However, a few months into my new role, I started to feel sick every day. I was always worried about things, feeling panicky all the time and suffering from stomach cramps and diarrhoea on an almost daily basis. I went to the doctors and was diagnosed with IBS — Irritable Bowel Syndrome. The more stressed I was, the worse my stomach would be and, of course, the worse my stomach was, the more stressed I'd become. It was a vicious, exhausting cycle.

I'd had a great relationship with my colleagues up until this point, but they suddenly noticed I was becoming withdrawn and no longer myself. I stopped interacting with friends and colleagues and became a recluse. I didn't know what was going on, or why I was feeling like this. Looking back, I don't think I realised just how much I'd changed as a person in such a short space of time.

It got to the point that I was always calling in sick, or I'd go home in the middle of the day because of IBS-induced stomach cramps or an upset stomach. I remember calling my mum from the bathroom, in floods of tears, having gone home with cramps, because I felt like I was going to pass out on the toilet. I don't think it's understood just how debilitating IBS can be and just how difficult it is to cope with.

After this particular incident, I went back into work and was greeted by my boss who told me I was lucky I'd returned to work, as I would have lost my job. Her words were harsh but fair, as I was letting the team down. There wasn't anything outwardly wrong with me, and I hadn't been diagnosed with anything 'serious', so I don't think anyone, myself included, really understood just how awful I felt... ALL. OF. THE. TIME.

It was a big wake-up call. I loved and respected my colleagues and the thought of letting not only them down, but myself too, made me realise I had to make some big changes. I sat down with myself and looked at my life and what I was doing. I realised that I didn't have many friends. The friends I did have, I never saw, because I would always make excuses for why I couldn't socialise. My weekends were literally spent in my room, reading online blogs or watching YouTube videos of people living the life of my dreams, or ordering things I'd never wear from ASOS.

I wasn't going out anywhere.

I wasn't doing anything because I was so afraid of the world.

I was letting the anxiety win.

It didn't help that the anxiety made my phobia of sick so much stronger. I have a phobia of sick, of people being sick, anything to do with vomit at all. It's not just that I don't like it, it's overwhelming, terrifying for me. I would create excuses in my head like, 'You can't go to the cinema because what if somebody chokes on some popcorn and is sick?' or 'You can't go to a restaurant with your friends because what if you eat some food, and you get food poisoning?' or 'You can't go on public transport because what if you're on a bus or on a train that's moving, and someone's sick next to you, and you can't run away?'

It was that fear of not being able to escape or the worry that something terrible was going to happen that controlled my life. I ended up not going out at all. It got to the point where I'd had a chat with my boss, and I was like, 'Wow, this is obviously a lot more serious than I thought'.

After that, I looked at my life, and thought, 'What the fuck am I doing?'

My first step was to come off the contraceptive pill. I'd been on it for about eighteen months, and to this day, I don't know why I made the decision to stop taking it, I just did. I didn't have a boyfriend at this point, and I wasn't leaving the house, let alone having sex, so it wasn't necessary. Within a week or so of coming off of it, I felt like a cloud had been lifted. All of a sudden, I was like, 'Oh shit. That's where the problem started.'

I still had the same fears, I still had the anxiety, and I still had the voices in my head telling me to be afraid of everything, but I also had this other inner voice, a confident one desperate to be heard.

A few weeks later, my friend suggested I join him and a group of his friends at a local pub that Friday. Again, pubs are places that I would avoid because obviously they are full of drunk people and in my head, all drunk people do is throw up everywhere. When my friend suggested I go, I was like, 'Do you know what? I'm gonna ignore all the voices. I'm gonna set myself a small challenge.' And this small challenge was to be in the pub from 8pm till 9pm.

On that Friday night, before it got really busy and jam-packed full of drunk people, I went in. When I got home afterwards, I was like, 'Okay, cool. 1-0 to me.' The following day, I couldn't stop thinking about how utterly brave I'd been. I was proud of myself for taking that first small step and knew that if I continued to take baby steps, I could turn things around.

It was hard to do. Terrifying, in fact, because the last time I'd been out in a social situation that involved a club or a pub was two years' previous, and somebody had been sick next to me. My flight or fight reaction had caused me to run across the street in front of a bus. Thankfully, it was far enough away not to hit me, but things could have been a lot worse. The fact I'd gone to the pub for an hour on a Friday evening was a massive deal. To knowingly put myself into a situation I was so afraid of, took a lot of guts and positive self-talk, but I knew it was something I needed to do.

I've always had the phobia of sick, and the experience of someone being sick near me exaggerated it. Everyone always said to me, 'Oh, nothing's gonna happen. It's fine.' But I'd had these instances, throughout my life, where it had happened in front of me.

Emetophobia is the medical terminology for it. It's something that runs in my family. My aunt suffers from it. My mum suffers from it. My mum has actually gotten worse as she's got older and I think constantly being around that, knowing that other members of my family were terrified of it, contributed to my own phobia.

My mum and dad divorced when I was around eight, so my nan used to pick us up from school most days. When I was eleven, I was coming home from school on the bus with my nan and my younger brother, Luke. It was always quite crowded. I was stood in front of a lady and all of a sudden, she was sick into a bag. Instantly I wanted to run. My stomach flipped, and my heart beat out of my chest. All I wanted to do was escape. I remember being so angry with my nan because she said to the lady who'd been sick, 'You're looking a little better now, the colour's coming back into your cheeks.' I felt so betrayed that Nan could talk to this woman who'd caused me so much stress and anxiety. It's funny isn't it, how your emotions work? Looking back now, the lady must have been so embarrassed and felt so lonely. Nan reaching out to her would have been a comfort to her. But at the time, I couldn't handle it.

The bus incident along with what happened at the club and various other incidents throughout my life, inevitably made my phobia worse. But it's one of those things: if somebody's gonna be sick, it's guaranteed to happen near me. It would never ever happen in front of anybody else, no matter where we went. My boyfriend teases me about it. He's a dive instructor so is often on a boat with his students and he's rarely ever seen someone vomit from seasickness, but one afternoon, as the boat was coming back to the dive school, I saw someone throw up over the back, and I wasn't even on the boat! Nobody else even knew it had happened. I guess it's funny really. Maybe it's to do with the law of attraction, and that you attract what you think about the most.

As I worked to overcome the anxiety and started to leave the house more, my friends were incredibly supportive. One of my best friends at the time was really encouraging. He would take me to the pub regularly and if I said no, he'd manage to convince me. Every time we went out, he'd stand with me. If I said to him, 'I'm really freaking out,' he'd be like, 'We're fine. It's just gonna be an hour. You're doing really well.' He wanted to bring me back out of my shell because he'd known me long before the anxiety had arrived. He knew that I was fun. I was a lot of fun. I was great at socialising when I was younger, but for some reason, I'd kind of forgotten that. The fear of someone throwing up outweighed the excitement of a night out with friends.

My friends were incredibly encouraging, and it got to the point where, as the weeks went by, I increased the time I'd spend in the pub. So, for a couple of weeks, I'd go to the pub for an hour. Then I'd go for two hours, and then I'd perhaps have a couple of glasses of wine myself. It got to the point where a few weeks later, I went from the pub to a club for the first time. All my friends had been doing this for years, and there I was at twenty-one, going to a club for the first time.

A couple of months after this, on a night out, I met a guy. I fell head over heels within a matter of weeks. We had such an intense relationship that came to an abrupt end after just three months. It doesn't sound like a very long time, but it was...it all happened very fast.

I met him in a bar two days before Christmas. We clicked instantly and spoke all day every day for two days. On Christmas Day, my friend said to me, 'You know he's got a girlfriend.' I was shocked and absolutely gutted because there'd been such a strong connection between us. I messaged him and explained we couldn't be involved romantically. I refused to be the other woman although, in hindsight, it would have saved a lot of pain all round if we'd just had an affair.

I saw him again a few days after Christmas on another night out with friends, and the chemistry between us was obvious. But again, I told him nothing could happen, and a few days later he split up with her. A week after, we went on our first official date, which ended up being both lunch and dinner on the same day. I told him he should enjoy himself and be single for a while as he'd been with his ex for two years, but he was adamant he wanted us to be in a relationship.

We flew away to Austria for a week of skiing just nine weeks later. By this point, we'd talked about marriage and kids, and he'd already said, 'I love you.' When we got back, we booked a holiday to Turkey for three months' time and started discussing the best type of mortgage for us. At this point, I was still only twenty-one. I'd only just started coming out of my shell but being with him made the process move a lot quicker. He'd take me to places, encourage me to go out and as a surprise for him, I booked us tickets to see Drake at the O2, never once worrying about the crowds because I was so focused on how happy it'd make him. I was so wrapped up in this perfect bubble of happiness that I never thought was possible for me. Then almost overnight, it ended. Suddenly and unexpectedly.

By this point, I was regularly going out on a Friday and Saturday night, and a couple of weeks after we returned home from Austria, I went out with the girls, and he went out with the boys, and we arranged to meet up afterwards. A standard Friday night. A few hours into our night out, I got this feeling in my stomach. I felt sick, my stomach flipped over and I had this horrible feeling of dread which appeared out of nowhere. It was my intuition, my gut instinct. I said to the girls I had to leave. No explanation, no listening to their pleas for me to stay, I had to leave. I got in a cab and called the boyfriend to find out where to meet him. He told me where he was and to ring him when I got there so he could come and meet me. Twenty minutes later, as the cab pulled into town, I called him. 'Stay there, don't get out of the cab. I'll come and meet you. Just don't get out of the cab,' he said.

Ever since I was little, if someone tells me not to do something, I have to do it. So, I got out of the cab and walked towards the club he said he'd be in. He was stood outside with his arms around his ex-girlfriend who was sobbing into his chest. Twenty-one-year-old me didn't know how to react. I was fuming, hurt, upset and terrified that he was going to get back with her.

That night he apologised, and told me that seeing her confirmed to him how much he loved me, and that he only wanted to be with me. We went home together, but when I woke up the next day, something felt different. I went back home, and on Sunday, he came to my house to tell me it was over. He wasn't over her and had used me as a distraction.

I was broken.

Completely and utterly broken.

People always talk about the pain of heartbreak and to be honest, I'd never really understood it until that day. It felt like someone had put their hand into my chest, grabbed hold of my heart, and wrenched it out of my chest. I couldn't eat, I couldn't sleep, I couldn't talk. I just cried. For days, for months.

I was head over heels in love with him, and he told me he was in love with me too. It wasn't just words, I felt loved by him. We had planned and talked about our future together. I just couldn't understand but at the same time, I felt like I deserved it. I felt I deserved the pain and the hurt because he'd split up with his girlfriend to be with me. This was karma, right?

And then it hit me. It was starting all over again. The anxiety, the fear of leaving the house, the constant worry. I told myself, 'Okay. I can't let this situation define me. I can't be the girl that's constantly crying at a night out or feeling anxious because of how somebody else has made her feel.'

I needed to do something to take my mind off it all and put the pieces of my heart back together.

For the first time in my life, I thought about travelling. I had a chat with my mum and said, 'This is something that I want to do.' She rolled her eyes and assumed it was just another one of those things I was excited about that I'd soon lose interest in.

My family and friends were shocked. I never did anything on my own so why on earth would I want to backpack solo? I never even went on public transport on my own. And even though I'd started going out with friends, Grandad would pick me up and take me there, so I didn't have to get on a bus. But the more I looked into travelling, the more I wanted to be as far away from the UK as possible. It was the only way I could imagine getting over him and dealing with the heartbreak. It was escapism. I thought running away from the problem was the best solution. No matter where you are in the world, if the problems are in your mind, they'll follow you.

I convinced myself I could do it and started to tell my friends, family and colleagues. Some were excited for me and encouraged me to go for it but most people didn't believe I could do it. But that fired me up even more and made me more determined to go for it. My mum knew I could do it. She said, 'Go for it. You can achieve anything you put your mind to.'

I intended to go to Australia for three months, but as I was sat in STA Travel, the trip evolved into an eighteen-month, round the world trip visiting South East Asia, securing a working holiday visa in Australia, and a few months back-packing in New Zealand.

Out of the eight flights I had booked, I only ended up getting on one. Not because I couldn't do it or was homesick or gave up after the first destination.

I fell in love.

I fell in love with Thailand and, later on, Tom.

I flew out to Bangkok in December, a week before my twenty-second birthday. I didn't want to be in the UK for my birthday because I still wasn't over the break-up. I couldn't handle the fact I wouldn't be with him on my birthday. Dad and my brother, Luke, dropped me off at the airport. Mum later told me that Luke's first words when he got home were, 'I really didn't think she was gonna get on the plane.'

Even on the day I went, nobody thought that I would do it. And yet, I ended up being away from the UK for sixteen months in the end.

I'd never done a long-haul flight before. The longest flight I'd been on was around three hours, and that had always been with someone. The eleven-hour flight to Bangkok felt like an eternity. There I was, thousands of feet up in the air, asking myself, 'What have I done? I don't know if this is the right thing to do.' I felt sick with nerves, excitement, fear, and anticipation for what was to come. I was on a plane full of people, thinking what if someone's sick near me? I'd taken a lot of travel sickness tablets before the flight so was hoping to just sleep the whole way, but I was too anxious. At one point, a stewardess came over to the lady in the row next to me with the oxygen tank, which obviously made the anxiety a million times worse because my first thought was, 'Oh my God, she's not well, she's gonna be sick.'

How I survived the flight, I don't know. I did a lot of deep breathing, chewed a lot of gum and turned my headphones up as loud as they'd go. I'd never heard of meditation or other anxiety-combating techniques at that point because I still didn't know I had anxiety – I just thought I was stressed.

I made it through the flight and landed in Bangkok where I was welcomed by a wall of humidity as I stepped out of the air-conditioned airport. It was a massive culture shock. I've returned to Bangkok many times since and that wall of heat, the uncomfortable humidity, makes me feel at home. My heart literally sings.

As I was getting my backpack off of the luggage carousel, I started chatting with a guy who'd also just landed. We shared a taxi to our individual hostels and swapped contact details so we could explore the city together the following day.

I checked into my hostel which, to this day, is one of the best hostels I've stayed in, and made my way up the three flights of stairs to my girls-only dorm. I got into bed that night and sobbed, thinking, 'What the fuck have I done?' I felt I'd made the biggest mistake of my life and eventually, the streams of tears sent me to sleep.

The first couple of days were physically challenging as I adjusted to the heat, and mentally challenging too, as I listened to the conflicting voices in my head – one asking me who I thought I was, believing I could backpack solo, and the other reassuring me just how brave I was, telling me everything would be ok.

The following morning, I woke up determined to make the most out of my trip. After spending the day with Danny – the guy from the airport – I returned to my hostel to find large groups of people socialising on the decking area outside. I felt so alone. I was intimidated by the crowds of happy backpackers and felt like a misfit for feeling so miserable when I was supposed to be feeling excited. I was still overcoming my social anxiety so instead of joining in with the conversations being had, I sat at one of the public computers to use the free internet. I logged into Facebook and started talking to friends from home. After about an hour, the absurdity of what I was doing hit me. 'Rebecca, you've come all this way, and you're sitting on Facebook. What the fuck are you doing? You might as well be at home.'

I had another one of 'those chats' with myself and said, 'Rebecca, you can sit here feeling sad that it isn't what you expected, you can cry about missing home, and you can stress yourself out about feeling lonely, OR you can get over yourself, grab the opportunity of a lifetime by the balls and make this journey AMAZING.'

I closed down Facebook, logged off of the computer, took a deep breath and went and sat next to this huge group of people. I sat there listening to their conversations and stories, and then someone spoke to me. We chatted for a while, and then I joined in with other conversations, and an hour or so later, I was stood on Khao San Road with a bunch of people I'd just met, feeling excited, happy and laughing my head off.

When I realised it wasn't down to anybody else but me to enjoy this trip, I knew I had to make an effort. I had to push myself, I had to ignore the voice telling me I couldn't. I knew if I pushed myself again, and again and kept repeating to myself, 'Come on, you can do this,' then I'd have an incredible time.

And I did. I had the most incredible experience.

Before my trip, I'd booked my first week of accommodation as I found comfort in knowing where I'd be for the beginning of the adventure. So, after a few nights in Bangkok, I travelled up to Chiang Mai with Danny. It was a fifteen-hour day train and a tough journey, not only because of my dislike of travel but because I'd only had one hour of sleep and was disgustingly hungover.

How times had changed!

By the time we got there, it was dark. I walked around for over an hour trying to find my hostel and when I eventually found it, there was no one at reception. A sign on the door said, 'Back in fifteen minutes.' I waited for half an hour, and nobody came.

I cried. Again. After an exhausting day of travel, an hour carrying my life on my back in the humid, 30-degree heat, all I wanted was to lie down and go to sleep. I'd spent five days building myself up, and now I felt like I'd taken two steps backwards. I was in a brand-new country and didn't speak the language. I was also five days into what was supposed to be an incredible trip, and all I could do was cry about how homesick I was, and how difficult it was to fend for myself. I called Danny in tears and asked him what I should do. He was staying in a twin room in a hotel and said I could use the other bed for the night and we'd figure things out in the morning.

The next day I decided I needed time to be on my own. Immediately, I felt like I'd failed. What backpacker goes and checks themselves into a private room? I'd become a 'Flashpacker' – often looked down on by 'I'll-sleep-anywhere-as-long-as-it's-cheap' backpackers. But I knew I needed to do something for me. When I asked myself what I needed, alone time was the answer.

I checked into a private room and spent two days doing my own thing. I slept late, got my nails done, sunbathed by the pool, went on a night safari and took a Thai cooking class. My focus needed to be on what would make me happy – essentially self-care before it became popular online. I didn't want to worry about what all the other backpackers were doing; that wasn't important. I needed to reflect on how I was feeling, rather than focusing on other people, because I'd spent my whole life doing that.

The group of friends I'd made in Bangkok travelled up to Chiang Mai for my birthday and after a few days of sharing a twenty-bed dorm with them, visiting waterfalls, viewpoints, drinking from buckets and attending Muay Thai shows, I travelled to Pai with Liz who I'd met in the toilets of the hostel. I'd never heard of Pai, and when Liz asked me to join her, I thought, 'Why not?'

What was the point in making this big, exciting trip if I wasn't going to be spontaneous?

After a week in Chiang Mai, we took the bus up to Pai. The three-hour ride took us up into the mountains and through 762 curves in the road. As someone that is not only terrified of people being sick, but who also suffers from motion sickness, it was another massive challenge, but I took some tablets and thankfully, I was fine. I actually slept for the whole journey.

When we arrived, we decided the best thing to do to explore was to rent mopeds. We told the guys at the rental garage that we knew how to drive them, and they gave us the keys. We must have driven twenty metres before stopping, and both said, 'I can't do it.' Neither of us had ever ridden one before, and we were both terrified. We decided to take them back and rent push bikes instead. We found it hilarious and just laughed at ourselves.

We decided we wanted to visit a particular waterfall. Looking at the map and based on what we'd heard from others, it would only take us around fifteen minutes to cycle to the base, and we could walk up to the top from there.

We took our map, 500ml of water and got on our little bikes. We cycled uphill for about an hour until we were in the middle of nowhere. We rode past two little huts in the middle of the wilderness. There were dead snakes on the road, cows roaming, and I thought, 'This doesn't look right. I'm sure it was only supposed to be ten minutes away, and we've been cycling for an hour. Where the fuck are we?'

By this point, we were trying not to freak out, and enjoy the journey, but there was something inside me screaming, 'Oh my God, what am I doing? I'm gonna die in the middle of Thailand. I've only just got here. I can't believe this.'

We carried on cycling, because what else was there to do, when a van drove past and stopped. We told them, 'We're looking for this waterfall,' and they said, 'It's another twenty-five miles that way.' We looked at each other, full of confusion and said, 'Twenty-five miles? That can't be right. It's only supposed to be ten minutes away.' We showed them the map, and they said, 'You're not even on the map anymore. You've gone way out.'

Well, we burst out laughing. I've never been able to read a map, but Liz worked in Wales where she took people hiking and climbing so how we managed to get lost I don't know. The couple put us in the back of their van with our bikes next to us and drove us to the base of the path to the waterfall. We cycled to the starting point where there was a 'bar' and were told by the bartender it'd take about four hours to get to the base of the waterfall and back again. By this point, it was about three o'clock in the afternoon, so we made the only logical decision: sit in the hammocks and drink a few beers.

As we were leaving the bar, I experienced one of my favourite memories ever of travelling. We walked across a little wooden bridge over this stream in the jungle. There were two children, a little boy, and a little girl, probably between the ages of two and five. They were playing in the stream, the happiest kids I've ever seen in my life, and all they had was this little bucket that they used to flick water at us. You could see they were just using their imagination to play the most incredible games. They were so happy, and they had nothing. And that moment, I constantly go back to throughout my life. I remind myself that you don't need anything to be happy as long as you're happy inside yourself.

I learned so much just seeing the sheer joy on these children's faces who had nothing. We went the wrong way, we were really hot, we were tired, we cycled uphill – which is bloody difficult in the midday heat – and we still didn't achieve what we'd set out to. We could have looked at it two ways: We could have felt annoyed about it, we could have complained, we could have felt frustrated, but we didn't. We made the most of it and enjoyed it.

Those lessons to me are really important, when you look at things and say, 'Okay, I don't need to reach this point for something to be a success,' or, 'I don't need to achieve this particular thing to feel like I've done something I should feel proud of.' It was a real eye-opener and was probably the start of one of the pivotal moments in my life when I reassessed what was going on in my life, and how I felt about myself and what I was doing.

The bar we'd sat drinking at was where I met the guy who told me to do my Open Water course with Big Blue on Koh Tao, and Big Blue is actually where I met Tom. Funny how things work out, eh? Had we never got lost, I might not have gone to Big Blue to be certified as a diver, and therefore I may not have met Tom....

I stayed on Koh Tao for a year.

I knew I wanted to be on Koh Tao for Christmas so after Pai, I said an emotional goodbye to Liz in Bangkok and made my way down to the islands. On Christmas Eve, after becoming a certified diver, we went to the bar and had a couple of drinks.

I woke up in my bed the next morning completely disoriented. I didn't know where I was. I didn't know what had happened the night before, where I'd been. My memory was totally blank. It was absolutely terrifying.

I'd drank two small bottles of Chang at the dive bar and ordered a bucket from the bar along the beach. I remember ordering the bucket, taking a few sips and then nothing. My drink had been spiked. I can't explain how horrific it is to wake up in your bed not knowing how you got there, especially when you know you hadn't drunk a lot.

I found out from the people in my dorm that I'd been found on the beach and brought back by whoever had found me. I was beyond grateful for the kindness shown by complete strangers. They protected me and made sure that, even though they didn't know me, I was safe.

After that night, I decided to cancel my plans to celebrate the New Year at a full moon party on Koh Phangan. I felt like I'd taken a step back. I was back to being frightened of my surroundings, feeling anxiety when I went out and worrying about what could happen. I didn't want to push myself this time, I knew what I really needed was to stay where I was, where I knew a few people, and again, ignore what every other backpacker was doing. I just needed to do me. And I had an awesome time celebrating the start of 2013.

On February 13th 2013, I met Tom.

I was in the dive school, sitting with the guy I was seeing at the time Billy, and his friend Greg. On the table next to us was a guy sat on his own with a cool-looking tattoo. Knowing how intimidating it can be to be on your own, I decided to invite him to join us. We got chatting and just clicked. A few minutes later, Greg turned to Billy and asked who the girl was that he'd been kissing at the bar the night before. Awkward doesn't even describe the atmosphere!

Tom and I got on like a house on fire. We soon had a solid group of friends and went on to live in the Big White House together. The first time something happened between us, I was still seeing Billy. Not ideal I know but I broke things off with Tom soon afterwards. Tom and I were never in a relationship, never a proper couple, we'd just hook up sometimes. We knew that we had this bond and this connection and this real deep friendship, but we never spoke about being together. We thought it was just an 'island fling'.

Three months after meeting Tom, I went on a visa run to Malaysia with my friend Dan, and it was then that I realised I was in love with Tom. All I could think was, 'What the fuck am I gonna do?' I couldn't tell anyone that we'd hooked up because I knew it would cause tension in our friendship group. I knew he still had hopes of getting back with his ex-girlfriend who was living in the States at the time.

Falling in love wasn't what I expected or something I was looking for, especially as I still wasn't over the break-up. But love isn't really something you can control, is it?

We spent eighteen months denying our true feelings for each other. Being so in love with someone but not able to do anything about it is hard. Really bloody hard.

Being in Thailand was one of the first times I ever really understood what true friendship was because although I had friends at school, I never felt I had anyone that I could tell everything to until I went travelling, and I met Tom and a few of my other friends from Koh Tao. We'd get home from nights out and sit on our balcony having such intense conversations about the world. We'd stay there until sunrise and then we'd order breakfast and go to bed.

Tom left after about ten months, and I went on to Sydney, Australia, which was my next stop. I was there for four months, but Tom and I spoke almost every day. He'd stay up until 2am to call me and I'd wake up early to call him.

Being in Sydney was a bit of a blur. It was challenging to start with because I missed my Koh Tao family and, of course, Tom. After just a couple of weeks, I got pneumonia and was admitted to hospital on Christmas Eve. If it wasn't for Elaine, a girl I'd met in the dorm I was in before I got pneumonia, I don't know what I'd have done. We'd only known each other for a few days when I got ill, but she came to the hospital to visit me every single day and even packed up all my belongings that were still in the dorm room. To this day, she's one of my closest friends.

Elaine and I had an incredible time. We partied a lot. We both worked in hospitality so our hours were similar and we just had a lot of fun. We were carefree, both sharing tiny flats with eight people and we just didn't worry about anything apart from which guy we fancied that week. A quiet dinner would always end up with us in a club at 4am doing Jagerbombs. It was awesome. I never went to uni but I feel like travelling gave me a taste of 'uni life' in a way.

After four months in Sydney, I flew back to the UK.

Within a couple of weeks, I met up with Tom again. When he picked me up from the station, the chemistry was obvious. It was like no time had passed, and we began seeing each other casually. Nothing too serious. He was living in Oxford, and I was back home in Essex. A few weeks after spending the weekend in Oxford with him – I'd been home for nearly two months at this point – and then I discovered we were pregnant.

We were absolutely terrified.

My intuition told me I was pregnant before I took the test. I remember sitting in my car and calling Tom. I felt sick at having to break the news to him. What would he say? How would he react? Would he ever speak to me again?

We spent weeks discussing what to do, travelling back and forth to see each other to try and work out what was best for us. It was a challenging time because I've always been completely against abortion. I always thought it was a selfish thing to do and that it was something I could never do, no matter what my circumstance. Tom and I talked about all our different options because, as Tom's dad says, 'We all have choices.'

Tom was twenty-two and I was twenty-three at this point. We were still incredibly young, and I thought, 'Okay, I've got the support of my family, they're all brilliant. They all said that they'll try and support us, and Tom's family have told him they'll be there for us as well. We can do this.' Our families were so supportive even though I hadn't met Tom's parents at this point, because we weren't in a relationship.

I decided I couldn't go through with an abortion.

But one Saturday morning, I was out shopping with my mum, and stood in Mothercare, staring at cots and prams and other baby paraphernalia. She was chatting away to me about 'baby this... and baby that' and I suddenly thought, 'I can't do this. I can't put myself through this. I can't put Tom through this. I can't put the child through this.'

I knew in my heart, I didn't want it.

And I knew Tom didn't want it in his heart either.

We had many more discussions and came to the conclusion that the best thing for all of us would be to terminate the pregnancy. We knew we couldn't bring a child into the world that we didn't want. What kind of start in life is that? Knowing that your parents didn't want you?

Having grown up in a home environment where my parents had divorced, where I felt like I was caught in the middle of their hatred for one another, I knew I didn't and still don't want that for any child I have.

We knew it was the right decision for the child. We couldn't bring a child into an environment where we couldn't support it financially, and we didn't have the capabilities to support each other. I would have resented the child because it would have been an obstacle in the way of Tom and me, and in the way of my life and his life.

It's a tough topic to talk about, and it's something that many people don't know, but it's something we shouldn't be ashamed of which is why I wanted to include it in my chapter of this book. I want people to know that it's not something you should be ashamed of and it's not something you should allow yourself to dwell on.

When I first went to the doctor and told her I thought I was pregnant, I said I didn't know what to do. Her words comforted me and are something I continue to remind myself of: 'Whatever decision you make now, is the right decision for you at this time in your life.'

And I honestly believe that.

Falling pregnant happened over four years ago, and it's something we'll occasionally discuss now. It's important to communicate openly with your partner. It wasn't a decision we made lightly, and we've never regretted it, but I just like to check in sometimes that he's still feeling ok about it. A lot of the time, when you make the decision to terminate a pregnancy, the concern falls on the woman's wellbeing. People don't always understand the impact it has on the man. Whilst the man doesn't experience the physical side of pregnancy, he still experiences all the emotions.

I've always said to myself, 'I'm not going to go back and question what things might have been like if I'd have done this or that.' It was our choice, and we've stuck to it. I've never looked at it as a regret. We've both said we could dwell on it, we could talk about it, we could analyse it, and we could obsess over whether it was the right decision, but that's not going to be helpful for either of us.

After the termination, we discussed what our next steps were going to be. We both knew that we didn't want to be in the UK, and decided to travel to Australia together. We wanted a fresh start and a chance for us to have a proper relationship. We didn't want to have made that decision and then just sit in the UK and not do anything with our lives. We wanted to make sure we were going to go out and live our lives, so our decision hadn't been made in vain.

We booked a flight to Perth, Australia and left the UK feeling excited about our new adventure. Having just experienced the pregnancy, and making the decision to terminate, Tom and I were still the closest of friends and shortly after arriving in Australia, we decided to become a couple. As we began exploring a new kind of relationship, we were thrown head-first into the most difficult three months of our lives.

As I was re-entering Australia on the same working holiday visa, I needed to find work on a farm to secure a second-year visa. At the time, you were required to complete eighty-eight days of rural work in order to extend your working holiday visa for another year. A week after we landed in Perth, we were offered a job on a farm in Mildura. With just over one-hundred days left of my visa, we thanked our lucky stars we'd found somewhere and booked a flight for the following day.

We were collected from the airport by a man in a white van and one of the other girls from the farm. As we got in the van, we were asked for our passports and $450 cash each. We'd been told about the fees before we arrived but needed to visit a cash point. Our passport details were taken down, and we were given a form to sign. Upon arriving at the shopping complex, we were told to withdraw our cash and buy enough food to last us a week or so, because we wouldn't be living near the supermarket.

As we made our way into the supermarket, we asked the girl what the farm was like. We'd heard so many horror stories about backpackers being taken advantage of, so we were naturally apprehensive about our stay there. She assured us it was ok and there was a good bunch of people there. Feeling more at ease, we did our shopping and were driven out to the farm.

The atmosphere in the van was frosty. We didn't know why but we both felt uncomfortable. As we turned right into the farm, we were given our first glimpse of home for the next three months. An area the size of a football pitch contained around eight caravans, an outside toilet, and an outdoor shower block as well as two small, portacabin-like buildings.

Tom and I were shown to a caravan that consisted of two single beds, a small wardrobe, and a DIY small double bed. This two-person caravan was to be the home we shared with another couple. As we unpacked our suitcases, we began talking to the couple, and they revealed the owner of the farm – the guy who'd picked us up from the airport – had been all over the news for exploiting backpackers. Videos on YouTube confirmed this was true, but we didn't have a choice but to stay – I had one-hundred days left to secure my second-year visa, and we'd just handed over $450 each to be there.

We had to stick it out.

We awoke at 5.30 am the next morning, freezing cold. While temperatures in Mildura reached up to forty degrees during the day, at night time, the temperature plummeted. The couple we were sharing with had left in the middle of the night, leaving us a note urging us to go too. Bleary-eyed, we got dressed and waited outside to be told what work we'd be doing that day.

Nothing. There was no work for us.

At the time, we took this as a blessing because we were both tired after the journey and were feeling unsettled in our new surroundings. We spent the day making friends with the other backpackers on the farm.

The small kitchen contained a basic oven with four ring burners on top, a microwave, stand-alone freezer, and large, double fridge. With at least thirty of us living on the farm at any one time, preparing meals was a challenge. People not washing up after themselves, using other people's food and making too much noise. Cooking led to friction and caused many an argument.

Weeks went by without us working, and while we would still get our visas signed off, we weren't making any money. Every two weeks, we were expected to pay the owner of the farm $300 each. It was illegal for him to charge us rent, so instead, he disguised what was essentially rent, with the title 'finders fee', claiming that this was our fee for him to find us work.

We were rapidly eating into what little savings we had and becoming more and more concerned about money. The owner of the farm had a split personality – some days laughing with us, and other days threatening to kick us off the farm and yelling abuse at us all. His temperamental nature meant we were scared to ask about work and instead, chose to keep quiet.

Each morning, we'd need to get up early to see if we had work. Often, we'd wait around for hours before he'd show up to tell us nope, no work today. It was exhausting. We were just thankful that we made such good friends while we were there.

Eventually, Tom started getting work here and there picking oranges and began earning $20-25 for an eight-hour day at work. When the owner of the farm came to me and told me he wanted me to work for him directly, I had no choice but to agree.

I needed to stay on the farm.

I became one of his 'recruiters'. We'd create ads on Gumtree advertising for farm hands, making false promises about earning $80-100 a day and saying what a wonderful place it was to be. My phone number would go on the ads and backpackers would call me up to secure their spot, at which point I'd have to tell them how amazing it was. I'd focus on how lovely the people – our friends – were and the fact that the hard workers could actually make that much money. We'd urge them to book their transport immediately and once we had confirmation, we'd add it to 'The Book' so we could go and collect them on arrival.

For every person that came to the farm because of us, we made $30.

If our ads on Gumtree were reported – which they often were – or we failed to get any new recruits, we'd be shouted at. We lived in fear. Would he be having a good day or would he go off at us for nothing?

I hated every second of it.

I hated the fact I was encouraging people to come to the hell I was living in. I hated the fact that these backpackers, who I was supposed to be on the same team with, were being exploited because of me.

But I needed that visa. I had to do it. Quitting wasn't an option.

After about a month and a half of being on the farm, I was unofficially promoted to 'favourite person'. My days were spent driving around in the van with the farm owner, dropping people at work, getting coffee, picking up papers from his lawyer, whatever he was doing that day. I became his PA. I even helped him fill out his accounts in this home.

The hardest thing in this whole situation was that there were times where I didn't hate this man. There were times where I actually enjoyed his company and was grateful for the fact that I didn't have to pick oranges, I just had to get coffee. He'd buy my lunch, buy my coffee and he even took myself and another girl out for a business dinner he was having.

It's still one of the most difficult times of my life to try and process.

While sat in the van with him, he'd talk to me about Tom. He'd ask me why I was with him, he'd tell me he didn't really love me and that he'd seen Tom talking to other girls on the farm. He'd seen him flirting with other people and knew he was going to cheat on me.

He told me I should be with him. I should marry him and have his twin boys.

The constant mental abuse from this man undoubtedly caused tension between Tom and I and between the single girls on the farm. Our relationship was still very fresh and to repeatedly be told that someone doesn't love you day in, day out, has a massive effect on your mind. I felt like I wasn't good enough. I couldn't stick up for Tom because that just made the farm owner angry. And I felt guilty for not sticking up for him.

Everyone believed I had it easy and couldn't understand why I was feeling so low. The only way to describe it is mental abuse. It knocked my confidence completely and began to drive a wedge between Tom and me.

About three weeks before we were due to finish our time on the farm, the owner got into an argument with Tom and forced him to leave. I packed my bags to go with him, but Tom told me I had to stay for both of us. We'd come this far, and I had to secure my visa so we could continue this new adventure together.

'Okay,' I thought, 'I need to do this for us.'

The owner agreed to let me stay, and in the weeks that followed, I did everything he asked. Tom spent a few nights in a hotel in Mildura before deciding to head to Melbourne to secure us an apartment and job before I'd finished at the farm. Knowing he'd be so far away made me feel sick, but I understood why he was going. I spoke to the farm owner, and he agreed I could stay with Tom the night before he left and say goodbye to him at the station before returning to the farm.

In the hotel room that Tom was sharing with our friends, I received a message, 'You need to be back tonight, you have work at 6.30 am tomorrow.'

I hadn't been given work for over two months. We all knew this was his way of controlling me and manipulating the situation. In his mind, he expected me to refuse and stay with Tom.

I didn't.

I wasn't going to let him win.

I took a cab back to the farm that night and cried myself to sleep. I got up at 6 am and was ready to leave for work by 6.30 am. 10 am rolled around and I still hadn't been collected. I was distraught. In the end, I was picked up so late, I could have said goodbye to Tom at the station before going to work. But I just got in the van, bit my tongue and took my anger out in the orange field.

A week before I left the farm, it was the owner of the farm's birthday. I organised a cake and a handful of presents from all of us. By this point, I'd learned that to survive, I needed to become his friend. I've always gone the extra mile in any job I've had. This would be no different. This was a job. I needed to view it like that to keep me going.

The night before I left, I had butterflies of excitement. The owner of the farm had asked me to stay on, offering me $30,000 in cash if I stayed for another three months. I politely declined. As we said goodbye at the airport, I felt like we'd reached a turning point. The mental abuse had lessened, and I no longer felt afraid of him. He told me to check my bank account when I landed because he'd deposited a little 'thank you' in there. I got on the plane and cried tears of relief. It was finally over.

I landed in Melbourne to find $2,000 in my bank account. I was stunned. I immediately messaged him 'thank you' and felt grateful that my time on the farm ended in a positive way.

Three days later, I received a threatening call from him claiming I'd stolen from him and he was going to get me back. The police contacted me about his claims, and I revealed everything to them. They'd heard stories about him before and said there wasn't much they could do. I'd already spent part of the money on accommodation and paid off the credit card I'd used while on the farm. I returned some of the money but was then advised not to send the rest back – it'd been given as a gift and was therefore mine.

Not only did the abusive calls from him continue but I soon started receiving messages from people I'd been with on the farm telling me he was threatening not to sign their visas because of me. It was a terrible time, and I spent my first month in Melbourne living in fear that he'd find me. My anxiety had returned, and I began having panic attacks again.

It was time for another one of 'those chats' with myself.

I had two choices: I could become the victim and live behind the excuse that I was the way I was because of him, or I could face things head on. I could forget the farm, secure myself a job and move on with my life. Tom and I could move on with our lives.

And we did.

The next two and a half years were spent living in Melbourne, Cairns and the UK where we moved back in with our parents and spent eighteen months living apart as we saved for our next adventure.

Six months after being back in the UK, I started having panic attacks on an almost daily basis. My stomach would swell up, almost as if being pumped up like a balloon. Within a short space of time, I'd go from having a flat stomach to looking four months pregnant. This gave me major anxiety, and I just couldn't work out what was wrong with me. I loved my new job. I had a good social life, and went on trips to Prague and Slovenia. I missed seeing Tom every day, of course, but we'd see each other every four to six weeks and would speak on the phone as often as we could. The more I tried to analyse myself, and the more I tried to work out what was wrong, the worse it got. I went back and forth to the doctors before being diagnosed with irritable bowel syndrome again, having been fine for five years.

The anxiety continued and was affecting my daily life. I couldn't cope with the panic attacks and felt myself becoming more and more withdrawn again. I'd have terrible mood swings and couldn't control my emotions at all. I spent my days worrying about all the things that might go wrong. I went back to the doctors, and I was referred for cognitive behaviour therapy.

I had six weeks of one-to-one calls that I found helpful. They taught me how to see things logically rather than getting lost in thoughts about things that were out of my control.

As the anxiety began to ease and the panic attacks became less frequent, it was time for our next adventure.

We were going to Utila, a small island off the coast of Honduras.

Tom was ready to train as a scuba diving Instructor, and I decided to use this opportunity to start my own business as a social media manager. Before we left the UK again, in February 2017, I'd set up my social media profiles as a 'Freelance Social Media Manager & Consultant'. I started receiving enquiries before I'd even quit my job and within a couple of months of being on Utila, I signed my first few clients.

And then the anxiety returned. Again.

Imposter syndrome kicked in hard, and I struggled to cope with the workload from the clients, I'd already taken on. I battled trying to secure new clients so I could make enough money to cover my bills. There were online social media managers making £2k, £5k, £10k+ a month, and there I was barely scraping £800.

Why was I not as good as them?

I began to self-sabotage, and listen to the imposter's voice in my head, comparing myself to anyone and everyone online. Even when I did sign a new client, I'd think, 'Oh my God, what the fuck have I done? I don't know what I'm doing.' Everything I'd learned during the CBT therapy had gone out the window. I hardly left the house, I didn't try to meet new people, I'd spend my days sleeping or crying. We'd only been living on Utila for a few months, but I hated it. I hated it because I felt like everything was going wrong.

And then an email arrived in my inbox one day that spoke to me.

It was from a coach who I'd signed up to receive a freebie from. Her words were exactly what I needed to hear in the place I was in. With promises of clarity in my business and helping me reach the £5k months I dreamed off, I took her up on her free, one-to-one strategy call offer. We talked for over an hour, and at the end of the call, she invited me to work with her. I signed up for her signature programme and began the three-month programme the following week.

During our first session, she introduced me to the idea of self-care and talked about mindset work. She encouraged me to take some time to myself and step back from my business for a few hours each day. I laughed. I had a mountain of work to do, how could I do anything other than work twelve hours a day?

But I realised I was burning myself out. I began to work on my mindset with positive affirmations, practicing journalling and meditation and then I realised the problem wasn't that I wasn't good enough as a social media manager. The problem was it wasn't what I really wanted to be doing. I wanted to be coaching people. I wanted to become a Life Coach.

Coaching had always been something I'd dreamed of doing, ever since I was a teenager. I remember looking at courses online and eagerly reading the free leaflets that came through the door about coaching certifications. I loved the idea that as a coach, I could help people.

At first, I looked at all the reasons I couldn't become a coach. At twenty-seven, I was too young. I didn't have a degree. What if no one liked me? What if everyone thought I was just a scam?

But then I had a conversation with my mum, and I realised that until I listened to what my intuition was screaming at me to do, I'd never be happy.

I hired a Business & Mindset Coach and began building my empire. Choosing to niche down to social media managers was terrifying in the beginning because, as with any new business, you don't want to turn away potential clients. But I'm so passionate about the work social media managers do and having experienced their struggles first hand, I soon began to trust that it was the path I needed to follow.

As a Confidence & Mindset Coach, I teach mindset work to social media managers so they can transform their confidence, overcome their fears of visibility and develop an unshakeable belief in themselves, their business and their abilities. Because when you believe in yourself, everything else falls into place.

My biggest ambition is to set up multiple rehabilitation centres for the homeless around the UK. Rather than just a shelter for them to stay in, it would be a full, six to twelve-month programme where we take them in, give them food, a roof over their head, and then encourage them to attend daily workshops on mindset, confidence building, life skills, and money management, so they can transform their lives completely. The workshops would enable them to be more employable and give them the support they need to make things happen for themselves.

I just want to help people, and while I do that in the form of coaching right now, who knows what's in store for me further down the line. What I do know is this, no matter what obstacles we're faced with, we have the choice to overcome them because, my dear, you can do anything you put your mind to.

ABOUT THE AUTHOR

Rebecca Hawkes is a Confidence Coach for Social Media Managers. When Rebecca launched as a Social Media Manager, she struggled to sign dream clients. She'd drop her prices, take on extra work and suffered from imposter syndrome. She had two choices: Give up or believe in herself. When faced with challenges, she always chooses option two.

After successfully landing multiple dream clients, doubling her prices and tackling the imposter, Rebecca wanted a new challenge. She knew it was time to follow her dreams of becoming a coach. Rebecca wanted to support social media managers in their journey so created a coaching programme focused on tackling the three main problems a SMM faces – pricing services, imposter syndrome and attracting dream clients. She now works 1:1 with SMMs to overcome these obstacles.

Rebecca constantly pushes herself out of her comfort zone. She's gone from being too afraid to leave the house to quitting her job, travelling solo and starting two online businesses. In January 2019, Rebecca's hosting her first winter 'staycation' retreat in the UK where guests will enjoy mindset workshops to increase their self-confidence.

Join her community The Become Your Best Self Club:
www.facebook.com/groups/becomeyourbestselfclub

REBECCA HAWKES

Confidence Coach for Social Media Managers.
www.rebeccalucyh.com

    @rebeccalucyh

Paulina Kapciak

CHAPTER 4
From Pain to Power
By Paulina Kapciak

"If you change the way you look at things, things you look at change."
– Wayne Dyer

You, my dear, are Stardust.

You are the Divine having a human experience.

You came here for a reason.

You have a mission.

And the moment you realise that, things will begin to transform before your eyes.

When you choose to take action, decide to go all in, the Universe will move very quickly to assist this transformation. It did for me. This sense of living for a greater purpose has accompanied me for as long as I can remember. A lot of it comes from being born at twenty-six weeks' gestation, weighing as much as a bag of sugar, with holes in my heart. Having spent the first two years of my life in and out of hospitals and knowing that I survived against such odds, has given me a huge sense of purpose. In the early 90s, it was really quite unheard of for a twenty-six-week, two pound preemie to survive. What I know for sure, is that I lived for a reason. I was given this life, this chance, and I needed to make something great of it. I didn't want to waste even a second of it. Even if your entrance into this world wasn't quite this dramatic, what I know for a fact is that you are here for a reason too.

This sense of having a greater purpose and being alive for a reason has always been there. Now I can honestly say I am living it one hundred percent. Today, I am a successful businesswoman. A female entrepreneur with an international passion-driven business, creating a life of purpose, freedom, and abundance. Today, I am helping mothers around the globe to create the same for themselves and their families. Today, I have a loving family and the home of my dreams. But it hasn't always been this way.

Less than two years ago, I was living my biggest fear. Coming from a divorced family, I had made a vow to myself to never put my children through a family break-up. Yet there I was, single, pregnant and with a toddler, moving back to my family home. I wanted to avoid this at all costs, because I knew the reality of living through a family break-up all too well. My parents divorced when I was ten, and it shook my world. As a teenager especially, it affected the kind of decisions I took in life. It affected my self-esteem, my self-worth, first relationships, and the way I wasn't claiming my power and stepping up to the massive mission I have in this lifetime. Over time, however, I realised I had a choice! I could let my external reality dictate my life or I could use it as fuel to propel me forward. As they say 'history likes to repeat itself', and fast forward to the break-up of my own family, I knew I wouldn't let it define me.

Reflecting back on my parents' divorce at this tough moment in my own family's life I remember thinking, 'What can I learn from this?' I realised that my mom really had to make a decision. She needed to make a drastic change in our life. She was a single mom and had been left with debt after the divorce so financially, things were really tough. She made the decision to emigrate from Poland to England. The fact that she made that massive leap, and drastic change to our lives, to shift things around and make things better for us, really showed me that you don't have to settle in life. You can always take control of your life and change things. You can always do something about the situation you're in. Her overcoming the circumstances, demonstrated the potential that we all have that power within to really create our own reality.

My mother moved to Britain first when I was just twelve and had to leave us behind for a few months. We stayed with her younger sister who was only eighteen at the time and in full-time education. She was away from home most of the time. My younger sister was only nine. It was hard growing up so fast. It definitely taught me to take responsibility at a very young age, because it was just my younger sister and me, which is crazy to imagine now.

Back then, that's the way it was, and I had no choice but to look after my sister, look after myself, make sure homework was done, that the house was clean and that we had something to eat each night. I had to pay bills, I had to learn about managing finances at a very young age. And as sad as it is to look back now and admit this, there was a time when there was no point in having our fridge on.

I am never one to be fixated on the past, so I rarely look back at those times. It feels like a different lifetime. I feel like all the adversity that I experienced so early on, I used as fuel to propel me forward. I have experienced that end of the spectrum and don't want it again. It's all about the contrast in our experience. It has then allowed me to understand exactly what I do want for my life. My mom took that big leap and improved our lives drastically, which has taught me that there's always something we can do. There are many options, and we can always shift things around. We can look at things differently and create our own reality.

We had lots of hope when we came to school in the U.K; it wasn't completely straightforward though. You can imagine, being in your early teens as a young girl, coming to a different country and not able to speak English very well. It threw some curveballs in the way. I actually ended up being bullied for a while by a group of girls. I didn't let it bring me down too much though. For a while, there was that tendency to hide my head in the sand and try to avoid school as much as possible, but I knew I didn't want to do that. I had big dreams. I wanted to shift things, so instead of hiding, instead of sinking into that victim mentality, I just decided to really move things around. It was so motivating for me to use my hardships as fuel. I had no doubt that I wanted to achieve amazing things. I didn't accept the reality I was given.

I ended up with amazing grades and offers from Universities, because I didn't let my experiences define me. I turned my obstacles into opportunities to rise to the occasion. I remember this one event, this big school event, where I sang solo, and the whole school was looking at me. I was up on stage and using my voice. To get to that point was huge for me. Everyone, including all the bullies, was so surprised because this timid, shy, immigrant girl was up on stage using her voice. That was really powerful for me. That was a huge sense of achievement, and again, another sign that things can shift, and you have the power to change things around despite your circumstances.

I guess you could say I was really geeky at school. I have always tried my best and wanted to achieve greatness in some form. I was the type of student that was always at the top of the class, doing all the extra-curricular activities, but I always felt there was a block, I had the sense that maybe I wasn't quite good enough, or that others were better than me. I think the fact that I didn't have a relationship with my father following the divorce played a crucial role. So, although I opted for business studies,

I had it in my head that maybe I wasn't quite cut out for business stuff, and at school, I felt like there was a lot of pressure on us to go a particular direction, for example, to do medicine. I knew I wanted to help others, that's for sure. I was fascinated by psychology and philosophy, and I always asked the big questions in life.

And so I went on to study Psychology at University. Then quit. Then started another Psychology degree after several types of employment. I never really stayed too long in one particular place. I always kept looking for that 'something'. I quickly learned that the mainstream nine-to-five lifestyle wasn't for me and then the entrepreneurial bug hit me! I started my first online business at eighteen; I didn't know much about business, and I didn't have a lot of start-up money.

Nevertheless, I decided to build an online shoe boutique, with absolutely no strategy in place. It didn't work out as you can imagine, but the experience stayed with me for years to come. I got my first glimpse of freedom. My parents always had their own businesses, and I was used to that lifestyle. You could say I am too much of a rebel to have it any other way.

After that, I feel like I used academia to hide my head in the sand again and not really work on my life purpose. I didn't quite believe that I could do great things unless I had a PhD. I thought I needed all these qualifications and courses, before I could even begin.

I always wanted to write a book. I'd even started a couple as a little girl. I had a blog, when I was twelve, back when the computers were massive, and you had to use the dial-up modem to connect to the internet. So those seeds were there, but it took me years to peel back the conditioning and remember what I wanted to do.

For a while, I tried to fit myself into that neatly defined box of an academic career. I became a Research Assistant for a Baby Lab at a local University and got accepted onto a prestigious Master's Degree programme in Psychological Research Methods. That was actually one of the most aligned employments to date, but still, it lacked the freedom, impact, and creativity I craved.

I also worked in mental health for a while, in a psychiatric hospital setting with adolescent girls. That was such a deal breaker. One of my biggest awakenings and darkest times in my life. But it really opened me up to so much awareness.

It was very traumatic, and I didn't expect it to be. In my head, I had it all planned out, the great relationship, degree, excellent paying job, plans of becoming a developmental psychologist.

But that just completely shook me up. It woke me up, and I've experienced things that are really hard to describe. You see, I'm an empath, and so I really pick up on people's feelings and emotions. It took me a while to learn to shield myself. But back then, being a nineteen to twenty-year-old, I really wanted to help people, even if it came at my own expense.

I witnessed things most people can't imagine. Repeatedly, every day for six months that I stayed at that job. It felt like a war zone. Fighting for other people's survival, being the person responsible for getting there on time to save them from ending their life. After a particularly traumatic event at work, I decided it was too much. I decided to quit and left. I went to a supermarket, and I had my very first panic attack. I never experienced one before, so I didn't know what it was. I literally thought I was dying.

This was my dark night of the soul. I had spent weeks really trying to piece it all together, make sense of the world again in terms of what I'd witnessed, what I'd seen, and how I felt, and what was happening to me. It was the darkest and scariest time in my life. For weeks I couldn't leave my bed, my house. I had a choice to make. Either sink deeper into it, and it was very hard not to... OR use all that I had in me to overcome that, to find happiness again, and feel like I could face the world again.

I turned to spirituality, and that's what saved me.

When I left university, I was introduced to meditation by my boyfriend at the time. And then I was introduced to a book called Conversations with God, by Neale Donald Walsch. I've always been a very deep thinker, and very philosophical.

But growing up in a very Catholic country, it wasn't a great foundation for a really connected relationship with the Universe or God. As a teenager, I felt a lot of resentment, and a lot of anger, you could say, with God. I felt alone many times, and like he didn't care about the obstacles I was facing. And I felt conflicted as to what I was allowed to believe. So as a teenager studying philosophy and ethics, I kind of turned away from all that for a while, and I said, 'You know what? I don't want any of it. It doesn't feel right.' I wanted to put God into a tiny little box, and sort of leave it and not even think about it. Put it into a neat little box with all that resentment because I didn't have the answers to it all and was always told to believe a certain way. I kind of rejected it altogether for a while.

When I was introduced to Conversations with God and meditation, I thought, 'Wow, it's everything I knew all along, but someone has finally said it, AND I was allowed to believe it.' And it made so much sense about the Universe and God not being all vengeful and not caring. Something shifted and I knew my obstacles and hardships were really blessings.

And so going back to my dark night of the soul... I went back to spirituality. The thing that saved me before but maybe I took for granted for a while initially. I mean, it was there in some ways up until that point, but it wasn't the core aspect of my life, which it totally is now.

Having panic attacks and anxiety really made me think about my life in a different way, and what it all meant. I turned to spiritual books like Doreen Virtue's Angel Therapy, Eckhart Tolle, Deepak Chopra, Rhonda Byrne – all the amazing spiritual books that have had a lasting impact on me. And I was just consuming it all. I was also suffering from insomnia for a while so I would just try and read to keep my mind off flashbacks. I turned to meditation and prayer again. I knew I had to. It was my only hope. At the time, I was scared to see anyone about my anxiety, I didn't reach out for any kind of therapy, and I felt like it was all up to me to get better. It was my only hope.

I had the feeling something was consuming me, dragging me down, right to the bottom. I realised that unless I did something about it, and fought, I would sink even further. I had to fight to not sink completely. I had to fight to really find happiness again, to make sense of the world again. And the spiritual readings have really helped me with that. Meditation has really helped me too.

Suddenly, it was like this new reality had been revealed to me. I saw the world in different terms, with more energy, depth, and more soul, rather than from my ego. And then things got a lot better. After that point, I really struggled with the idea of going back to full-time work. I felt like I really wasn't cut out for that, even more so than before. Being in busy places was a cause of anxiety for a while. I did get an admin job to get by, but this time I would use my free time reading spiritual texts. I was also studying part-time again. At that point I fell pregnant with my son.

That was the game changer again. That was a huge realisation. From the day he was born, maybe even at some point, throughout the pregnancy. I knew I had a calling, and this mission, this sense of greater life purpose was all consuming. My intuition skyrocketed massively, and all of a sudden, I was getting all of this inner guidance. It was unquestionable. I couldn't ignore it and get on with other stuff. And I knew, especially after David was born, I wanted to lead a collective change of some kind. That was the beginning of being on the right path.

I found myself being totally in the flow of that intuitive side of me, and before my son could even speak, I was picking up on so much communication from him. This, more often than not, contradicted with the plethora of external advice I was given as a young mom. I was being told all these things by our society and the people around me, but my intuition was telling me that wasn't what my son was communicating to me. Things like, being told the very first thing you need is a cot and that you should let them 'cry it out' or not pick them up every time they cry as to not spoil them. Instinctually, I felt like I needed to have him next to me in bed, and he was very much communicating that as well. I realised I don't have to use punishment and harsh discipline, but connection instead.

After a while, I realised that I didn't have to listen to all this external advice. All I have to do is really trust my intuition and trust my son, and what he was communicating to me. And to really not be afraid to go against the mainstream in how we do things. We would go to all these baby groups, and I felt very different to everyone else. I felt quite lonely in the first couple of years bringing him up so differently from the mainstream.

After a while, I connected with a few other ladies who shared this similar sense of intuition or divine guidance when it came to children. And that's when I really began blogging about all this stuff. I started building a community of women who wanted to be a parent in that sort of attached, conscious, spiritual way. And to listen to those instincts and their internal guidance. It was really incredible; it finally gave us a place where we belonged. It reassured us that we're not alone.

Realising that other people shared similar experiences, values and beliefs, was really amazing. That motivated me to do something about it, and to connect with other moms, and support them more, because even though we found this community, there were still things they really struggled with as mothers. There was alienation if we weren't surrounded by a like-minded tribe, or self-doubt and guilt, if you spent even a minute on yourself, or did something other than focus on your little ones; there was overwhelm and burn out, when you're constantly giving so much, and you don't take that time for self-care.

I decided to use what has helped me to overcome my anxiety, and the spiritual tools that I picked up along the way, to support those moms inside our community. It's all interwoven into our community, so there's a lot of support. After a few months in business and very rapid success, many of the mothers in my community felt inspired by my story to follow their own dreams. It was then I expanded into business mentoring, because I discovered that it's not just me who has this sense of mission. There are thousands of conscious mothers out there with a mission in their hearts. Whether that's around conscious parenting, healthy eating, spiritual healing, reducing toxins or environmental impact. I realised all these moms have that in common. They are thought-leaders, visionaries, change-makers.

They are raising babies and businesses that are changing the face of our world. They are stepping into their life purpose, and it is so powerful because they are each listening to the Universe and the guidance that they're receiving. They are stepping into that life purpose and finding the courage to do it, to go against the mainstream, to pave a different way, and create a completely new world.

I feel like the moment we become mothers, we find these enormous creative powers, huge amounts of resilience and leadership. All of which are beneficial to the creation of impactful conscious businesses. Motherhood brings so many life lessons, it really can be the quickest spiritual catalyst out there. It's a catalyst to becoming who we really are and who we are meant to be. It's like we suddenly remember and we find the courage to step into our power. We birth a baby into this world, and we suddenly remember our divinely creative powers. We are a channel between the divine and the material worlds. We are a vehicle through which souls travel and come into this physical plane.

A new era is here for women in business. Our divine feminine aspects such as intuition, empathy, connection, collaboration and leading with love are more than ever before needed in our world, and our businesses, today. Mothers make the perfect conscious visionaries and business owners of today.

Soulful, spiritual entrepreneurship is the way forward. With mothers at the forefront. So, after years of wandering about, trying to seek clarity, I finally know what I came here to do. I finally know MY Mama Mission. It has been one steep and often messy learning curve, to not be afraid to step into my life purpose. I really want to support other moms who have a mission of their own to not be scared of that. It's our nature to want so much for our little ones. That we feel like we always have to give 200 per cent, with all eyes on them. While I feel like, yes, children have to come first, it's also incredible for us to have a greater sense of purpose in the world and to actually model to them that we can transform our society, that we can achieve beautiful things and create a collective change. We do not need to hide our powers or put our head in the sand anymore.

Mothers often feel like they're undervalued and their work goes unrecognised, but it's only the limits that we place on ourselves that holds us back. There are always things we can do to change our situation. Society might be designed a certain way, regarding that nine-to-five lifestyle, but we can make our own rules. We can build our own empires that work around OUR values and our family. Businesses that are expansive and provide time and money freedom. That's why I am so passionate about helping mothers to create freedom lifestyles that not only impact the world, and help them find their true passion, but actually create time and financial abundance too.

I would love to see a day where all moms can really follow their passions, dreams, and missions, while having their little ones next to them along the way. This is really an important message for me to share, that you don't have to be limited by the fact that you are a mom. It can actually be incredible for the little ones to witness as well. To observe all that impact, to see the self-love, and to witness a happy fulfilled mom day-in and day-out. Being a homeschooling mom, I always take my boys with me every step of the way, so I know that if it's possible for me, it is also possible for you.

We are moms on a mission. We are united on this collective path to creating a new generation. It's like a ripple effect, and we're contributing and creating this completely new world and taking our little ones with us along the way. It's the mama bear in us that's driving this. The mama bear who wants to create a better world for future generations. Our protective instincts are behind this. We know our world is ready for a rise in consciousness; we are prepared to shed the old and bring in the new.

For me, it took a drastic family breakdown to step into my big girl shoes and into my life purpose. It was the precise thing that I needed at the time to wake up further. Before that point, I wasn't really stepping up and showing up. There was no immediate urgency. I was relying on others to take responsibility. This showed up as me writing a random blog or article, maybe once a month, but not really pursuing it on a grander scale in the way that I could. To become the person that I was supposed to be. Being a single mom for two years, gave me that final push to step into my purpose on a big scale. It was perfectly orchestrated — the precise events I needed to step into my power.

By no means was it an easy decision, but it gave me that final push to make me step up, to not play small, because I had no choice. And yet again I was at the crossroads. This time asking... Do I play small and accept that societal narrative of what it entails to be a young single mom? Or do I step up and create a new version of reality, one that I know I really want for my family?

Can you guess which option I took?

I had to really step into big girl shoes, and really take responsibility for my life and for my finances, which were all over the place for a while. I had to heal codependency and to begin being responsible for my life.

This was when I decided to put my degree on hold for the second time to pursue my business. I had to make that decision to go for my dreams because at that point I knew what my message and my life purpose was. I was a pregnant mom with a toddler, juggling employment and a degree AND now I knew I wanted a business. Not just any business, but one that moves and shakes our world. I had to make a decision to yet again put my studies on hold. To make a quantum leap and start my business.

It's like I suddenly remembered what I had to do. It's not even that I had to, but it was so exciting, and I had this fire in my belly. I kept on working on all these ideas in my head. I had a choice: do I explore this new idea or do I continue with the studies? I decided that I had to make that huge leap to follow my dreams and to share that message the way I wanted to.

Yet again I turned to books and self-development and consumed information about what it would take to build an online business, and to spread my message on a large scale. This time, yes, I had the spiritual aspect with me, but it was also business-focused. I knew I could step into my purpose, create abundance and help others do the same. I would not let my obstacles define me. I would build my own reality on my terms. Because I felt like no one was coming to my rescue and nobody would create this life for me, I had to own up to it. I really had to take responsibility 100 per cent. I feel like so many women around the globe are going through that right now. Women who are passionate to step into their power and responsibility and create lives on their terms.

And just as I got to the other side of this life lesson, our family was reunited once more. Universe, I got the lesson! I listened. The unimaginable happened, and we healed despite the two years of separation. We are definitely wiser and stronger as a result. It has changed us in ways we could never have predicted. I honestly didn't think we would ever be here again, together as a family.

I've come to believe that all my past misfortunes or apparent 'obstacles' were actually laying the foundation for the life I have now. They were OPPORTUNITIES. Each apparent obstacle really is an opportunity in disguise. A chance to rise to the occasion and peel back the layers of conditioning, layers of who we are not. All my experiences were necessary and crucial for this perfectly imperfect unfolding.

Yes, I was that shy immigrant girl who couldn't speak English for a while – but this propelled me to aim for greatness.

Yes, I struggled with trauma and anxiety – but this allowed me to embrace spirituality which now is my rock-solid foundation in every life area.

Yes, I became a University 'drop-out' TWICE, but this has allowed me to search for a deeper meaning and not conform to the mainstream.

Yes, I was a 'single mom' for two years, but this has allowed me to step into my power and create freedom and abundance for my family.

So yes, I could let the obstacles define me. I had that option, and it would be very easy to. But the rebel in me knew to look for blessings. The non-conformist in me made a decision to create my own definitions and reality instead. I turned my biggest pain points into power.

YOUR circumstances, YOUR past or present situation does not have to define you either.

Everything is happening for you, not to you.

It's time to claim back your power.

It's time to do what you came here to do.

ABOUT THE AUTHOR

Paulina Kapciak is the founder of MomTribe and a mentor for Mamas on a Mission from around the world.

Having become a single mother whilst pregnant with her second son, she has made a radical decision to abandon her post as a Research Assistant and to decline a Master's degree in Psychological Research, in order to fully turn her passion for conscious parenting into a flourishing business. She set out to create world-impact, and decided to live a life of her dreams, on her terms.

Her work has immediately sparked great interest and within just a few months it has been featured on Ariana Huffington's Thrive Global, major in-person events and podcasts, and she has been named as a Woman to Watch in 2018. Since experiencing exponential growth and success, she now empowers and mentors other mothers to fully step into their life purpose and to create world-impacting 6 and 7-figure businesses.

PAULINA KAPCIAK

Founder of MomTribe and a mentor for Mamas on a Mission from around the world.

 @momtribe.co

 Mama Tribe (private group)

"Even the bravest of creatures have some fears but it is not enough to stop them from moving in the path they are destined to walk upon."

– Anonymous

Kate Bollanou

CHAPTER 5
Rise and Lead your Life!
By Kate Bollanou

"I want every little girl who's told she is bossy, to be told instead she has leadership skills."
– Sheryl Sandberg, Facebook COO

Looking back at my life I realise that every difficulty I've been through has made me stronger. It's not easy to have this perspective when you're in the situation, as feelings like sadness and anger dominate. But as you go through the cycle of emotions, you finally reach a point where you see the lesson you've learned. You no longer feel the pain. You are wiser because you were forced to become. You then take this wisdom and move on with your life, trying to avoid mistakes of the past.

At least this is what I try to do. I fall, and then I get up again. And I've fallen quite a few times already.

I was born and raised in stunning Athens, Greece with my mum, Joie, and my father, Konstantinos. My grandmother and my Aunt Jenny, who's like a second mum to me, were around when I was born.

One of my earliest memories was going to nursery with my mum and hopping around a few steps ahead of her, totally carefree. I always felt so loved and cared for and never could have imagined that changing. Sadly, my parents got divorced when I was four and a half years old. The transition was very smooth, and I suppose I didn't understand the enormity of what was really going on. Both my parents and my stepfather, Babis, made it very easy for us all, and that really is testament to the wonderful people they were.

A couple of years later, my sister, Alexia, came along. I was delighted. I adored my siblings so very much and wanted to hold and kiss my baby sister all the time, she was adorable. My brother, Paschalis, and I would see our father quite often after the split and went to his house every weekend.

In the meantime, my aunt and my grandmother moved away. My grandmother went back to the Philippines, and my aunt went to Sweden to have her own family. One of my strongest memories is when my siblings and I used to play together. My brother used to love teasing me to the point of tears! When I think about my childhood, I always have feelings of adoration for the bond I had with the two of them.

I grew up in a beautiful place called Palio Faliro. It's close to the sea with a long stretch of golden sand, and we had a play park close by that we used to go to every evening in the summer holidays. It was so lovely and just feels like a completely different era. Back then it was more laid back, my mum would let us take the bikes and go around the area without her supervision, and it felt utterly safe. I used to tell my parents that I would never move away! Little did I know!

My life up until I was about nine-years-old was quite normal. I was happy at home and saw my dad often. We would go on holidays together like every family does. We went a few times to Serres to visit our relatives, the place my dad was born in. There was a particular freshness in the air, combined with the beautiful smell of cherry blossoms, that whenever I come across now, bring back sweet memories. I never got to meet my grandparents from his side, but I was delighted to meet the rest of the family.

Sadly, when I was about nine and a half years old, my dad passed away. He had leukaemia. That was an incredibly heartbreaking period of my life. I found it difficult to comprehend what happened. I thought that I would see him again when I grew up.

I still remember the last time I saw him. It was an evening after school, and my mother bought me some crisps and toy cards. My dad was lying on a bed in the living room, unable to talk or sit up. I felt scared to talk to him. I knew he wouldn't be able to respond. I didn't know that would be the last time I saw him.

He had been sick for a long time. We would sometimes go to the hospital together. Sometimes nurses would come to his house to give him his medication and his injections. My parents had never told us what was truly going on. I guess you can't say the whole truth to such a young child. I thought he just had a cold and it would eventually go away.

The following day my mum called me and Paschalis to the kitchen, burst into tears and told us the news. It all felt like some sort of awful blurred dream. I was devastated; although I had lost my father, I didn't lose my father figure. I had my stepdad by my side. I always had his support and love, and he helped my brother and me through our loss with such grace; it's something that I will never forget. I know for certain that if he wasn't around it would have been much, much worse. That is when I started calling him 'Dad,' instead of Babis. It came from my heart, it never felt forced.

About a year after my father's passing, my parents managed to buy an apartment in a newly-built building further down the street. It was spacious, brand new and it was ours; it was so exciting! I quickly picked which bedroom I'd share with my little sister, and I'd imagine what our new furniture would look like and how our new life would be in that house.

However, there was one sad thing that we didn't share with others: we had no electricity for one and a half years. My mum had to wash our clothes inside the bathtub and cook every day with camping gas. We would go home after school, have our lunch and do our homework before it got dark as we only had candles for light. My sister was about four-years-old at the time, and we would turn on the radio and dance with her.

I recently asked my mother why we didn't have electricity. She told me that the builder would not allow the electricity company to make the connection until we paid off the entire mortgage. I asked her whether he knew there was a family with three young children living there and she said, yes. I was shocked! Who does that? My father had to work very hard to be able to pay off our house and support a whole family by himself. After more than a year in this situation, my aunt found out and helped my parents financially. We finally got electricity!

Things outside my home were confusing. It was at that time I began to realise I was a bit different. I come from a mixed-race family, and that wasn't common in Greece. In fact, even these days Greece is not as multicultural as England. Children would continuously ask me where I was from. This experience made me very self-conscious as if there was something wrong with me. I became so tired of explaining my background to everyone.

Now that I have children of my own, I understand. Most of them were just making an observation; they didn't mean anything bad. What was a one-time observation for them, for me was something I heard every day. I felt I had to educate them, but I ended up being defensive of my identity. I'm half Greek and half Filipina, but I was born in Greece and raised with Greek values and traditions. Greek was also my first language. Despite this, people would still point out that I looked different.

Secondary school was more enjoyable as I had a big group of great friends.

I have been friends with my very best friend, Eleni, since primary school. We were very close and had such a lovely time together. We didn't have smartphones, and all the luxuries children have now. It was so innocent. We were twelve-years-old and quite naive. We would go out, talk about our dreams and drink hot chocolate. We didn't wear any makeup, but would sometimes secretly take our mothers' mascaras and lipsticks and try them on. It was very sweet, and I hope so very much that my girls get to experience that.

At the age of fifteen, I chose which subjects I wanted to take on for my last years in secondary school. I picked the more academic path and studied Ancient Greek and Latin. I wasn't sure what I wanted to study at University, but I was drawn to those subjects. At that time, I wanted to become a journalist. When I first came up with that idea, I was about twelve-years-old, and I remember calling the Greek TV channels asking how I could become a reporter. I often wondered how they even took the time to talk to me. We didn't have internet or emails, all I could do was call them. I would tell my loving English teacher, Mrs. Chrysa, about my dream: 'I'm going to become a CNN reporter when I grow up!'.

When I was sixteen-years-old, I got a job in the local video club. I was working there at the weekends and during school holidays. I loved the fact I was making my own money, and I could meet new people. As I got close to the end of secondary school, I changed my mind. I wanted to travel. I liked being in a fast-paced environment, so I decided to go for hospitality. I passed all the exams and went into the Institute of Hospitality where I studied for five years. It took me a bit longer to finish as half-way through my studies, I paused them to relocate to Dubai for an internship in Burj Al Arab. It was very luxurious, like nothing I could ever imagine.

I discovered this magnificent hotel on a flight to the Philippines, when we had a stopover in Dubai. My mother had a friend who lived there, so we stayed with her for a few days, and she took us to the hotel for an afternoon tea. When we came back to Greece, my dad suggested that I should apply to work there. I thought I didn't stand a chance, but he very wisely said that I had nothing to lose. That really sparked something in me, so I decided to go for it!

After approaching a chef I knew, I asked him whether he had any connections in the hotel. He sent an email to them, and eventually, the training manager answered. He introduced me to her, and she gave all of the details of how I could apply for an internship. I didn't care about the money, I just wanted to work there!

The moment I started the process I was one hundred percent focused on that. I wanted it with all my heart! To cut a long story short, I applied the first time and got rejected. I was so disappointed that I got a headache. All I wanted was to get my foot in the door. Being slightly stubborn, I wrote back to them and asked what went wrong, so I could correct it and apply again.

That made a massive difference, and it was the moment I realised that this kind of attitude could move me forward! The training manager seemed surprised and gave me a few tips to amend my CV. I applied again, and they offered me a six-month position as a Food and Beverage intern.

I was so excited! From the moment I got accepted in March until the start of the internship in July, all I could think of was that! It was the highlight of my hospitality career! I was working minimum six days per week, ten hours per day. I was only twenty-one, so I had lots of energy.

The hotel was breathtaking and very well-organised. I had already worked in the top hotels in Athens, but this was on another level. The employees took pride in working there. The training I received was beyond comparison.

Once a week I would take a day off. I had to take my bulky laptop, walk to the mall and go to a café so I could connect to the internet and email my family. Every month I would work in a different department, and that gave me the opportunity to meet even more people. I found it so interesting learning about other cultures.

Before leaving for Dubai, I hadn't told any of my classmates or my co-workers. Only a couple of very close friends of mine knew where I was going. I only announced it to my professors on my return.

Coming back to Greece I experienced big disappointment. I was sure that with this experience on my CV, I would definitely get a better position. But the answers I got from the HR departments were that I was too young! Once again, I felt discriminated. This time because of my age.

I couldn't see the future I wanted for myself in Greece, although I truly loved hospitality. I discussed all my options with my parents and made the decision to move to England. After about three years of trying to make it work, I finally changed direction and went into Shipping, like the rest of my family.

But when I arrived the UK, I felt I was taking a step backwards. I fell into the trap of comparing myself to my friends on Facebook. All of them were about my age and were progressing in their careers. They were managers, travelling the world, doing stuff that I wanted to do. I felt stuck in a small room studying. I felt like zero, and it was taking its toll on me. It felt like I had made the wrong decision.

However, I stuck it out. I was determined to finish what I started, despite my many tears. I found the classes very challenging and the projects even harder. Fortunately, I had my classmates' support, as well as Leif's, my professor's guidance. Andreas, my partner, was my rock at home. His patience and his way of motivating me kept me going.

My classes finally came to an end, and although almost everyone went back to their countries for the summer, I decided to stay. My husband had already found a job in London so that was a good reason for me to stay too. While doing the dissertation, I found myself once again alone in a flat, trying to study for something I didn't feel suited me. I managed to submit in September, and everything went well.

I spoke to Leif about the opportunities I had in the shipping industry. He explained what a shipbroker does, and I felt that was the one! A good job that pays really well; I was finally going to shine! After submitting the dissertation, we went to Greece for a short break and straight after we returned, I began applying for jobs. The days felt endless, and I started doubting myself again. It got harder when no one was replying my calls and emails. After a month, I managed to land a job as a trainee shipbroker in a shipping company.

My parents and sister flew from Athens to Southampton to my graduation. There I was, ready to go on stage to receive my Master's, looking at my family with a big smile on my face.

'I made it!'

I was so proud of myself! I had just graduated and I had already found a job. I couldn't wait to start my new life!

This moment also marked another transition of my life. It was when Andreas and I moved in together. I was so in love with him and couldn't wait to make it official!

Andreas and I had met a year before while working in a Japanese restaurant in Athens. We were just colleagues in the beginning, and we both had partners. After a few months, our relationships came to an end, and we started dating. Things were not as smooth as one would imagine. It took some time to settle down into the new reality. It wasn't straightforward, but we both had to try hard for the relationship to work. We chose each other every single day, no matter what life threw us. And here we are now, married with two lovely daughters.

That restaurant was the last one I worked for and the one that I have the best memories from. That's where I also met my soul sister, Ioanna, who now lives in Los Angeles with her fiancé. It was also the place we met our best man, Marinos, and his wife Maria, as well as Kumi and Tony, the parents of my goddaughter, Mio. Although we all live in different countries, I'm very close to all of them.

The shipping company I started working for was a small family business, and all the employees were British. It was completely different from the big, multicultural companies I was used to. I knew it would be challenging at times, but made the decision to give it a go. The Directors were very supportive of me. Unfortunately, that new environment came with its challenges...

I was the youngest, the only foreigner, and the only female broker. It wasn't too long before I became self-conscious of all these. I needed some time to adjust, as I couldn't bond very well with the rest of the team. They would joke around, and I couldn't understand them. British humour is different from Greek. I felt different...again. In one specific incident, I was sitting across from a lady, and she kicked the rubbish bin with her foot. 'I kicked the bucket!' she said, and everybody started laughing, apart from me. It felt awkward, and this kind of thing happened regularly.

Shipping is a male-dominated industry. I used to go to meetings and networking events, where I was one of the few women and usually the youngest. Men would hardly ever speak to me, and as I was usually with one of my directors, they very often mistook me for their assistant. That really affected my confidence. At the same time, I always felt that I didn't know enough to join the conversation myself, so I wouldn't even take the initiative to discuss with them. That was my imposter syndrome kicking in. Feeling like a fraud, feeling inadequate.

My solution to that was to gain credibility with my qualifications. The more, the better. And the more I had, the better I could justify to others (and myself) that I deserved my position and my salary. I studied for my professional qualifications during my employment there and became a member of the Institute of Chartered Shipbrokers. It took me a couple of times to get it right. As my company was sponsoring me, I had to tell my director every time I didn't manage to pass. I was so embarrassed, but his reaction left me speechless: 'It doesn't matter, you'll get there,' he said.

There were also situations where I faced sexism. When I joined the company, my colleagues expected me to make coffees for our guests, even though this fell under the admin team's responsibilities. I raised the matter to my directors, and that stopped. Women were also the ones doing the dishes. I once had a big argument with one of my female colleagues about this matter. I told her that we should all take turns, but her response was that the men were working really hard! How did I expect to be treated equally when the women themselves perpetuated these outdated stereotypes?

During my third year in the company, Andreas and I got married and were also expecting our first child. I was over the moon! I was getting married to the love of my life, and despite the fact I was diagnosed with polycystic ovary syndrome, I managed to conceive naturally. Then, we had some bad news. My sister was admitted in hospital.

We didn't know what she had, and although she went to numerous doctors in Greece, no one could give her a definite answer. She then had to have surgery in Germany, and I was planning to fly over and visit her. My mother wouldn't let me go and as she knew I would get upset and she was very right to do so.

I went on maternity leave and gave birth to my daughter, Penelope. After I gave birth, my mother and sister would visit every three weeks. I never questioned the reason. One evening I went to my bedroom to breastfeed my newborn girl, and Alexia asked me if she could join us. She then told me that after her operation in Germany, the doctors confirmed that she had cancer. She was almost twenty-three at the time. I couldn't digest what I just heard, and burst into tears and asked her whether it was over.

She told me that she had a couple rounds of chemotherapy left and then everything would be fine. I didn't know how aggressive pancreatic cancer was and how rare it was for young people like her, or how pancreatic cancer symptoms appear when it's usually too late to treat. There came a point when they couldn't travel so often. My sister was getting very tired and needed her medication.

When Penelope was six months old, the two of us went to Greece. We stayed there for forty days so my mother could help me with the baby. I also wanted to finish my shipping qualifications, so changed my exam centre from London to Athens. I spent most of my time with my sister and my mother, and in the evenings I squeezed in a few hours to study, while my mother would take the baby out for a walk. Once I managed to complete my qualifications, we flew back to England.

The trip from England to Greece became our new normal. We had a break in the summer because my sister moved to Crete as she was trying a natural approach for a few months. It was around August when my sister's health started deteriorating. My maternity leave was also coming to an end, so I had to contact my directors and explain the situation to them.

Things took a turn for the worse. I received a call from my dad saying it was time for us to come back and spend some time with my sister. I felt chills down my spine. I could tell from his voice that I shouldn't expect much.

It was a tough time for all of us, but mostly for my sister. She fought hard. She was very brave. Her cancer spread to her liver, and there was no way back. We spoke to many doctors, and there was nothing they could do. She had to go into palliative care. My father's cousin owns a private clinic in Athens, and we managed to get her in so she could have the best care.

Before Alexia went into a coma, we managed to spend some time together. I will never forget that day. We had all gathered to honour her, to show her how much we all adored her and to say goodbye. I can still close my eyes and see her beautiful face. She was tired and sad. But at the same time, she was happy, as she knew the pain would soon be over. As I write this, I feel the pain inside my heart. Tears stream down my face and there's nothing that can fill the gap she left. We were very close, we were best friends. I was losing a part of me, I could see the future we were planning to have together, drifting away.

My turn came, and I got to make her smile one last time. I told her everything she already knew... how much I loved her and how much I was going to miss her. I couldn't pretend anymore that everything was going to be ok. That's what we used to do because that's what she wanted from us. But not that time.

As everyone got to spend a few minutes with her, we sat outside her room. The doctors came, and it was time for her to be transferred. She entered the lift, and as the doors closed, I could see her holding her tears back. Silence... 'I love you!' is all I could think of and hoped that somehow she could feel it and take strength from that.

She went into a coma, and we were told she only had a few days left. After saying goodbye to my parents, we flew back to London. Once we landed at Heathrow Airport, my parents called my brother and told him the news. Our sister had passed. We were waiting for a minicab to pick us up, feeling devastated. I didn't know what to do. How to react. Although I knew it would happen, I was in shock.

It was the 10th of October 2015. The following day was my daughter's first birthday.

We tried to be as normal as possible. My brother was staying with us, and we had a small cake to celebrate her first birthday. We were still in shock about what had happened. Everything felt like a bad dream.

We flew back to Athens for the final arrangements. Even on the day of her funeral, I was in shock. I could see my sister laying in front of me, but I still couldn't believe what had happened. I couldn't cry. I had frozen.

It was her wish to be cremated. As this is uncommon for Greece, my parents had to drive to Bulgaria and fulfil her final wish. We had already returned to England. When they came back home, they brought my sister with them. Her ashes are in our house, inside a beautiful sealed box. On top of it is a bracelet I gave her a month before she passed. There were two hearts, one was for her, and one was for me. Our bond is eternal.

As hard as it was, I tried to go back to normal. I went back to work, and Penelope started nursery. Our daily routine kept my mind and my body busy. Once again, my husband was my rock.

In the meantime, one of my directors retired, so his son took over, along with his wife. The team changed too, and I ended up being the one who was the longest in the company.

The environment in the company also changed. It became more positive, and I was more confident. Things were better, and I felt happier. A year later I fell pregnant with my second daughter. I was delighted. But I realised I couldn't continue working for someone else with two young children and no family around to help us. Plus, I had finally admitted to myself that shipping was not for me.

One thing I learned from my sister's passing was that life can change from one moment to the other. It made me realise that I shouldn't take anything for granted and that I should live authentically. I was unhappy at work, and no matter how good my remuneration was, it wasn't what I was meant to do in this world. I had to stop wasting my time thinking that I would disappoint my parents if I left shipping. I had to take matters in my own hands!

I decided to hire my first coach to help me with this process.

At the same time, the shipping market wasn't doing well, and the company was going through a bad phase. I got so stressed, to the point I couldn't sleep, and my hair started falling off. I freaked out. I went to the doctor, and they confirmed I had anxiety and it was work-related. As they feared it might affect my baby, they gave me two weeks' sick leave. On my return, we took things easier. After all, I wouldn't put my baby and myself at risk.

It was Easter 2017, and we went back to Greece to spend some time with my husband's family. On the first day of my return to work, my director told me that they had decided to make me redundant. It was a shock for the rest of the team, and Andreas never thought this would happen. After all, I had been with them for almost six years, I was six months' pregnant, and my directors were very religious. But I knew. I could feel it. Since the day they realised I was pregnant, things changed. I say 'realised' because I didn't have the chance to tell them. I hadn't hit the twelve-week mark yet when they came to ask me if I was pregnant. Was that proper? Definitely not! Should they have waited for me to announce it when I felt ready? Hell yes!

Deep inside I knew it would happen. I wasn't shocked at all. I was rather prepared for it. I was already in the process of thinking what I could do, so I took that as a sign that things happened for a reason. I actually believe I manifested it! I really wanted to find a way out, but my plan was to create something of my own, and then once it had taken off, I would quit. I guess the Universe knew better!

My passion for women empowerment grew, even more, when I realised I was about to become a mother of two girls. Instead of wishing my child to be healthy, people wished for my second baby to be a boy. When I very proudly announced it was another girl, they asked me if I would have a third one. How infuriating! You see, Greece still holds on to old-fashioned traditions. Boys carry the legacy. Boys will continue the family's name. It's my job to do whatever I can to stop discrimination against girls. It's my job to raise my daughters to become strong, independent and happy women.

At eight months' pregnant and with a baby almost ready to arrive, I decided to retrain as a Coach. This way I knew I would be able to work for myself and care for my family the way I wanted to. By being a Coach, I could also help other women with similar experiences find their voice and step into the powerful woman they have within them! Ten days after completing the first stage of my Coaching training, I gave birth to Alice.

I paused my studies and resumed them when she was about three-months-old. In between my sleepless nights, feeding her and trying to figure out how to manage a very energetic toddler and a newborn, I was studying.

I won't lie, there were days I felt completely exhausted. At the same time, I felt the burning desire to complete my certificates so I could finally focus on building my business. My whole vision was taking shape.

I dug deep inside me to find the root cause of the difficulties I had faced in my life. I could see a pattern: I've always felt that I couldn't speak up. If I spoke up, it was considered disrespectful. I was too worried that people would be disappointed in me, that I'd be judged and rejected. You see, I was raised according to all these standards. It's very common in Asian cultures. Being a good girl was the ultimate goal. The kind girl who always smiles, the one who never disagrees and who shows respect to the elders. The one who dresses appropriately, speaks properly, and has the right friends. Let's not talk about boys... the ideal situation would be if I could marry my first and only boyfriend. Obviously, this didn't happen, and it was for a very good reason!

I won't deny that this was probably a personality trait to begin with. But putting this trait in the right environment, you can either enhance it or reduce it. My upbringing enhanced it.

Taking this further, I could see how it affected me as an adult. In my personal life, there were situations I wasn't happy with. But as I was trying to keep everyone happy (typical people-pleaser), I made myself miserable! I couldn't set healthy boundaries. It felt like everyone could step all over me, and I gave them the space to do so. I was too reluctant to stop behaviours that bothered me. I was also hesitant to even ask the cleaners to do their job correctly. I was too unwilling to speak up for myself when someone was insulting me. I would either pretend that everything was okay, or on rare occasions, I would lose my temper instantly. Sound familiar?

Going into my professional life, there were many times that I felt mistreated. In one of my first jobs, I let my employer humiliate me. I was only nineteen and wasn't aware of the fact that we weren't allowed in the hotel premises after our shift had finished. My employer saw me and asked if he could speak to me in private. I followed him a few metres away from everyone, and he started screaming at me from the top of his lungs. Everyone could hear him! I felt completely humiliated, I was shaking. I can't even remember what he told me, as once again, I just froze. If only I dared to stop him, walk away, or even swear at him! It would be much better than putting my head down and allowing him to do that to me.

I was overlooked for promotions and pay-rises and was treated like a little, clueless girl. The more it happened, the more I felt myself shrinking. If I had built my leadership skills, these would have been prevented. If I had the confidence and the courage to voice my opinions, things would be different. If I had the tools to present and carry myself with more authority, I'm sure I would have progressed faster.

So, there it was! That's the problem I was going to solve!

So many women play small because of all the fears inside them. All the cultural and gender stereotypes that suffocate them; all the 'shoulds' and the 'musts' from their environment. This has to stop!

My goal is to create a movement of women ready to rise up and get the life they deserve. Women who are fed up being the good girl, trying to please everyone. Women who are ready to step into the shoes of the strong, independent woman they've been hiding inside them. Women who are ready to take ownership of their life!

My North Star is the vision I have for my family: I want to be able to spend quality time with them. I want to have time with my husband. I want us to create memories, travel the world and be there for each other. It's not easy living abroad with no family around. We don't have the usual Sunday lunch with the family or an evening with the grandparents so Andreas and I can go for a drink. We have no one to help us with the kids when we get sick and need to take some rest. But that's what makes me want it even more. My business success will give me the family life I want.

I transfer my message to both my corporate clients and my one-to-one clients. With my corporate clients I'm able to provide them with a combination of coaching sessions and workshops on developing their leadership skills and foster an environment of inclusivity. When working with individuals, the coaching is more tailored to the individual's needs. But the end result is the same: Empowering women to speak up for themselves and be more assertive.

After all, change can happen one person at a time. I'm starting this movement by stepping into the strong woman inside me. Now it's your turn!

KATE BOLLANOU

Executive, Leadership Coach and an advocate of women empowerment.
www.katebollanou.com

   @katebollanou

ABOUT THE AUTHOR

Kate's mission is to help professional women from multicultural and male-dominated industries build their leadership skills, so they can successfully move to the next level in their career.

Kate's bi-racial background has given her firsthand experience of the challenges a woman faces while trying to navigate between two cultures, without losing her own identity.

Her first degree and career were in Hospitality Management. This gave her the opportunity to work in several luxurious establishments around the world, with people from different ethnicities.

In 2010, she decided to move to England and study for her Master's in Shipping and Commercial Law. Fascinated by the opportunities this country could give her, Kate decided to stay and pursue a career in London.

She worked as a Shipbroker for almost 6 years and during that time, Kate and her husband welcomed their two daughters.

While pregnant with her second child, Kate was made redundant. Wasting no time, Kate felt that this was the perfect opportunity to take the leap and retrain as a Leadership Coach.

Kate uses a dynamic approach that helps her clients position themselves better for leadership, by speaking their truth powerfully and with clarity.

Kate believes that all women can reach their full potential, no matter where they come from and what career they have chosen. One of her biggest goals is to be able to show as many women as possible that they can take ownership of their life, exercise authority and have confidence in themselves.

In her free time, Kate educates herself about conscious parenting, healthy lifestyle and nutrition. She loves staying at home with her family and sometimes manages to go out for dinner to try different cuisines, although she strongly believes her husband's cooking is way better than any fancy restaurant. Unfortunately for Kate, their 4-year-old also believes that 'Daddy cooks better than Mummy'.

"Our work should equip the next generation of women to outdo us in every field. This is the legacy we'll leave behind."

– Rupi Kaur

Megan Frasier

CHAPTER 6
A Woman Determined to Rise
By Megan Frasier

"Nothing that lasts is accomplished quickly. Nobody's entire legacy is based on a single moment, but rather the collection of one's experiences. If you're lucky, your legacy will be a lifetime in the making."
— Rachel Hollis

I grew up with visions of what my life would hold. Being an only child, I felt the pressures of having to be 'perfect'. Ticking all the boxes so to speak! Getting a good career, finishing college then getting married, starting a family.

I grew up in Walla Walla, Washington. A tiny, quaint, picturesque town, which is very close to my heart. I still get homesick even now. I lived there for the first seventeen years of my life. It's known for its sweet onions, wheat, wine, and rolling blue mountains. It's also a Christian, Seventh-day Adventist community (SDA), and so many businesses close at sundown on Friday and do not re-open until sunset on Saturday. There's a cute little downtown with shops, boutiques, and eateries. We have festivals, farmers' markets, and parades. It's a safe environment, with a small-town feel. Everyone knows everyone.

As I am an only child, my parents made sure that I had what I needed and put me first in their life. They have always made me feel special, wanted, and important to them. Even when I went through the typical teen frustrations, or they had the regular parental gripes, I have always respected and appreciated them. Now I admire them.

They are full of wisdom and always have my best intentions at heart. We talk on the phone, Facetime, and send messages often. I absolutely love to spend time with them whenever I can. We help each other in many ways, and I try to make sure that they know I love and appreciate them. At times it's really hard being away from my family.

No matter what I have wanted to do they have always helped me. They have always been supportive and encouraging. I played volleyball in elementary school and high school, and they were there at every single game. It didn't matter if I was scoring a point or sitting on the bench, they were there. They were always cheering for me and making me shirts or posters, and they still are my biggest cheerleaders.

In college, I had to work hard to be able to afford my undergraduate and graduate schooling, which was entirely self-funded. And, although I received small scholarships for my grades, it cost me hundreds of thousands of dollars, because education costs a fortune in the States.

I personally made many sacrifices to get through school.

After undergrad, I studied for my State boards and became a registered nurse. At that time in the States there was a shortage of nurses but to get a job in a hospital they required several years of experience. It was challenging for new graduate nurses to get a job at the time. (This stands out in my mind as one of my 'girl boss' moments).

One day I put on my favorite dress and wrote down a list of several nursing facilities that were close to where I was located, printed out my resumé and decided to stop by and see if anyone was hiring. I got a job on the spot and began that next week as a nurse on the floor. I didn't know much about it, but it was a sixty-bed, locked-down mental health facility. I guess people were taking bets when I started my training that I wouldn't come back and would be too scared to continue working there for long, after all, it was a very challenging position.

I did go back, and I learned so much during my time there. Within two months in the position, I was promoted to the Resident Care Manager and then a few short months later became the Director of Nursing of the facility. I worked there for several years before beginning my journey to bedside nursing in a hospital, just as I had always dreamed about. I hadn't planned to work in administration, but it certainly shaped my career and has given me so many opportunities.

I am a very hard, honest worker and treat people with respect and kindness. At the very, very young age of twenty-one, I became a leader, and ever since have been required to show courage, authority, dignity, and grace. It was then that I learned how important it is to lead by action and example versus having a title or a position. These experiences have given me such a foundation for my business as well; I will forever be thankful for this.

I met my ex-husband when I was seventeen. I was moving to the big city for nursing college and passing through his town. We kept in touch and later started our relationship. He was in the army. A sharp, sexy, stunning man in uniform. I was young, and I was infatuated with his charm and smooth words.

But, he was not always kind.

In fact, I felt like I needed to earn his affection at times. I had only had a few serious relationships before him and was still developing my self-confidence.

There were many signs that he wasn't right for me. But instead of addressing it, I said to myself, 'Maybe... if I changed, if I was better, if I did more, if I loved him more'... I could make the relationship better.

When I was twenty-one, he was deployed to Iraq. I remember I was so in love then, so fearful, so anxiously waiting. So worried.

Always waiting for a call, a letter, or a message.

I found out that during that time there was infidelity – and from that point many things in the relationship became unrepairable. It's hard to explain. I don't wish him ill, but it was a tumultuous time. His actions caused such a reaction from me – someone I am not proud of and do not recognize, someone I had never been and have never been since.

He had an addiction to alcohol and often lied about other things – and when trust is not in your relationship, it makes things very difficult.

I soon realized the issues were bigger than us. Serving in Iraq, he suffered from trauma and loss much bigger than I could fix. This caused a lot of self-doubt and self-sabotage on my part.

I was so afraid of failing, and I wondered if something was wrong with me.

Being a nurse, I thought that if I helped him get 'better' or, 'oved him more' maybe everything would be perfect. But, as the years went on, so did the toxicity in the relationship. The infidelity, trauma, and alcoholism, escalated into verbal and mental abuse, which got worse and worse and led me to question my value and worth.

He would always tell me that I wasn't good enough, that I wasn't smart enough, that I was worthless. I really struggled with that, and my negative self-talk grew. So many of my own fears and anxieties stemmed from that, and I didn't really realize it. It was a trauma for me.

Sadly, I knew that it was time to end our marriage.

I was worth more.

My life was worth more.

I knew that I didn't want to be unhappy, to be crying, and to be suffering inside. That's not a life anyone should be living.

I recognized it was toxic.

And as scary as it was for me to 'be on my own' or to feel like a failure, I knew it was something I had to do for myself and that my life would not be over if we divorced. Sometimes we'd argue over the silliest, nit-picky things. We did have good times, but they often led to alcohol-induced disastrous endings.

Some people witnessed his behavior. Like his friends we went drinking with. Some even stood up for me in certain situations.

I remember sitting with my head in my hands crying once, thinking, 'This cannot be happening. This is not my life.'

The very last time I saw him was a night that I would not like to relive. It was truly terrifying for me. I think that since I had endured his behaviors for years, I didn't react as I should have to the event that occurred that night.

The next day I traveled home, and that was the day that I made the decision to file for divorce, and I have not seen him since that time.

When it came to telling my family or his family about what was going on, I felt a sense of shame and failure. He was a very private person, and wouldn't share things easily. I would always tread lightly and say very little. I do miss his family sometimes, but I knew I had to do what was right for me. My friends knew a little bit about what was going on during that time. I just thought that if I showed him more love, that it would get better, but things did not change. Maybe it was the nurse in me. I was so upset as I had made a commitment and a vow. I thought in my heart of hearts that things could be perfect but it got darker, and I got lower and lower.

Despite this trying time, I have been fortunate and blessed to grow up with the same group of best friends since first grade. I have amazing parents and a fantastic family. They have always been so caring and so supportive. They always stand by my side, with kind and uplifting words, and have been there when I have needed them the most. I have also been so fortunate at my job at the hospital to have such kind and considerate co-workers who would also help to raise my spirits. Who you surround yourself with makes all the difference.

After the divorce, I moved out of my home and was on my own once again. I moved into a condo community that was filled with neighbors that became like a second family to me. They helped me in many ways. They were always there if I needed anything. We would have community nights, bonfires on the beach, go out on adventures together, have dinners. During this period, I was feeling a bit lost, but also really finding me again.

I was always keeping myself so busy. I didn't really take the time to or have the time to, I guess, sit and cry about what was going on. I was like, 'Okay, this is what's going on, I'm getting out of here, and I have all this stuff I need to do, and I can do this.' I didn't even take the time to grieve or process what had happened. Divorce really is like a loss or a death. But I just kept doing life, doing work, doing school, doing me, spending time with friends, going on trips, adventuring, seeing the world, kind of going through a bit of a wild, adventurous phase for a bit as well.

Friends my age (early/mid-twenties) were always going out, going to parties, etc. At times it was hard to say no. I was still finding my way, learning to step into my own confidence and discovering what my true priorities were, but I had to focus on studies and work.

I was committed to graduate school – I was in the midst of a four-year program to become a family nurse practitioner. I worked my nursing job at night and worked in clinic sites during the day for school. And in my spare time, which wasn't much, I completed homework and slept.

As part of my graduate course, I had to fly to the school once per month for in-person testing. We had written tests and exams called 'OSCES' (observed structured clinical exams). For my very first in-person test, I practiced and studied endlessly. I was up all night and trying to stay awake all day poring over medical books and reading my intricate notes.

I was so nervous. I could feel panic surge through me, and as the exam came to an end, I was given the news that it was a disaster.

The professor told me we would either pass or fail, no grades in-between. When she said I had failed, but couldn't tell me why, it seemed unfair. I didn't know if I'd got the diagnosis wrong, or the treatment plan wrong. She said I needed to retake the exam, and if I failed again, I would fail the class. I couldn't retest until the end of the term, so it was utter turmoil for me.

It was all I could think about every single day.

It caused severe anxiety. I cried for days. I hated not doing something well, and it also brought all-consuming fear — that I wouldn't pass. When I took the exam the second time, I was one of the only students to get a 20/20 score; I was absolutely elated.

Once graduate school had come to a close, this was when things began to slow down a bit, and other things started resurfacing. Anxiety resurfaced because I needed to study to take my State exams and I was fearful from my previous experience with the OSCE. Self-sabotage surfaced, in the form of words like, 'I am not good enough,' and they hit me like a block. Words that still lingered in my head from my professor, and from my ex-husband.

It was a tough time for me. I had growing anxiety, self-doubt, grief, and sadness. I had sunk to a low place. I had never experienced anxiety and depression like that before – and didn't want to acknowledge what it was.

It was during that time that I was really forced to sit down and process everything, to work through that anxiety and the negative self-talk.

Life had been so full on before, that I hadn't taken the time to process what was going on around me, including the recent loss of my grandfather, which hit me hard during the previous months as well. I tried to be strong and present for my family, but I also needed to take time to do nothing and to mourn and grieve. I ended up putting myself on the back-burner each and every day. I did what I could do to just 'get by'.

Needless to say, my negative self-talk was at an all-time high.

And my 'self-love cup' was totally empty.

Going through a divorce half-way through graduate school was not ideal. I was ridden with anxiety around my State boards, mainly because of that one failed exam and the experience with my professor. But I realized I knew my stuff, and that it was the anxiety holding me back. I had to completely refocus my mindset and created rituals for studying differently, rather than just hitting the books.

Before this, I had never felt that way in my life. I had the voices, and experiences from the past playing in my brain – from the professor, from that exam, and from my ex-husband, and I was becoming less social and trying to study; it was hard. I was so fearful of failing the exam. It was really when I started to prepare for the exam and began shifting my mindset that everything started improving, and in other areas in my life too.

It was at this point when I decided, once and for all, that enough was enough. It was a deep, dark, low point in my life when I realized I had lost who I was entirely. I am generally a very happy, loving and giving person, but at this point, I felt empty, numb, and utterly exhausted.

But, I knew I was going to step into my power, and into my light.

This was the beginning of my own self-love journey. When I really learned to say 'NO' to people and learned to slow down if needed. I found ways to be proud of myself and make myself happy. I didn't need others to be happy. I was doing things for me. I chose to not let others hinder my self-love and self-worth and learned to stand up for myself. After I had my period of 'grieving' I felt powerful and 'UNSTOPPABLE' which was very rewarding. Through the highs and lows, I never gave up. I always knew what I wanted, what my passion and desires were and that I deserved 'more'. Once I aligned with my true purpose, it seemed that everything began to fall into place.

Since these experiences, I have grown so much as a person, and I am continuing to grow, and become wiser as I get older. I have also taken the time to reflect over my accomplishments, and the things I have done – things I was told were 'dumb, not worthy, not smart, not good enough', but I did them anyway. I realized I was smart, worthy, capable, and strong enough to achieve every single thing I've ever wanted and dreamed for myself.

Every desire, passion, or idea I've had, I've declared, written down, made a plan for, and achieved. No matter how hard or scary, or how many times people told me it was impossible....

I have made it possible for myself.

That was my turning point, and that was when I knew I was powerful.

I am not small.

I began to heal.

In the midst of my tempestuous relationship, I decided to rescue a dog and bring him home from the animal shelter on a whim.

His name is Coco, and the thing is, in all honesty, he was the one to save me. He had been severely beaten by a previous male owner. The first day I brought him home he ran away. I was devastated; we searched for him for days. He was so scared. During his great escape, he bit a police officer and was on house arrest for ten days. I was just happy to have him home. After that, I hired a behaviorist and worked with him nearly every day for a year. It took time, and he had his moments, but I never once thought he would bite me. I often got down on the floor and hugged him, snuggled him and wrapped my arms around his neck putting my face right by his face. He could have snapped my face right up, but he didn't. He just loved me right back. It took him some time to befriend other dogs and other humans, but he eventually did, and now he is the sweetest, most loving dog. He has been by my side through thick and thin.

He is resilience.

I am resilience.

We have been through so much together. Over the last year, he has had a back injury. I have stayed up with him many nights when he has been hurting, just as he stayed up with me through so many nights hurting, studying, and wondering if I could ever be me again.

I believe everything happens for a reason and I was meant to find and rescue that dog.

After my divorce, I went on dates with a wide variety of gentlemen. Wild, dangerous, nice, safe. All types. I wanted to get a good idea of exactly what I was looking for. No settling this time around. One fellow, in particular, had asked me out for quite some time, nearly a year. It seemed our timing wasn't right...we were always taking trips at separate times. Also, he was older, and I wondered if it would make a difference. He was nice, quiet, kind. I was just not sure. I was also scared. We had mutual friends, so I did not want to ruin it if it didn't go well. I continued to go on other dates. I even went on dates with someone who had been in the NFL. It really made me see that money, fame, and looks, aren't everything, because if you're not happy and content with yourself, and if you're not kind, sincere and do not truly love yourself, then none of it matters.

When I was ready, I accepted the date with the kind and patient man and our timing could not have been more perfect. It was so magical, sweet and nurturing, and not like my past relationships. It was a genuine partnership. It's true that everything happens in divine time.

I spent that following summer and winter after school really focusing on me. Learning to believe in me and building myself back up, finding myself again. I dove into personal development, self-love and self-care practices and learned about new techniques to make me whole again from the inside out.

I learned about crystals and their healing properties and filled my home with essential oils. I began to learn about meditation and practiced each morning. I would often take my practice to the beach near my home. I implemented a gratitude practice and a bless and release practice into my morning ritual. I ordered countless card decks and practiced 'card pulling' each day to fill my morning up with positive affirmations. I saged my apartment to cleanse any negativity and have a fresh and clear space. While I was studying, I put rose quartz and citrine in my study space to infuse love, wisdom, abundance, and joy into my soul and mind.

I reconnected with my health and nutrition and took the time to slow down, enjoy each moment and to really get in tune with what gave me purpose. I got back to working out and moving my body. I got back to meal prepping, taking care of myself as a whole person, and remembering all the things that I loved about me. We are so lucky to live in the beautiful Columbia River Gorge, so I filled my days with hiking, waterfalls, and nature and truly took the time to enjoy the beauty surrounding me each and every single day.

This is what 'filling my cup up' looked like for me during the beginning of my self-love journey. I began journaling throughout my journey to self-love as well. I have never finished a journal before, and I completed several journals cover to cover. I poured my heart and soul into those pages and let things go. I also went on a lot of long walks. I walked to the beach where I lived and turned the music on and let it completely transcend me. I got the love of music from my dad. I listened to audiobooks and read a lot of personal development books and put my toes in the sand and let the water wash over me and cleanse my soul. I spent time with my Coco, my family and my friends and those that were closest to my heart. I nourished my soul.

I am a family nurse practitioner – in the US they also call it a 'mid-level provider'. I work in family medicine, similar to a family medicine doctor. I am a primary care provider (PCP). I have completed a total of eight years of college and graduated with my Master's degree last year.

I manage patients' care, diagnoses, write prescriptions, and am currently growing my panel. It's a bit overwhelming at the start taking on so much responsibility and realizing that you're managing people's care in all aspects.

I recently moved from Portland, Oregon to Olympia, Washington to accept an NP position and learn how to step into this new role. This was shortly after I began my business, With Love, Megan. It was right after all the challenges were settling down – which was another challenge in itself, learning a new career, moving to a town and not knowing a soul, and taking on new responsibilities.

That's my current day job outside of my coaching. It is a newer career for me; prior to that I was a registered nurse for eight years. With that knowledge and background in healthcare, nutrition, health and wellness, and my true love for taking care of yourself every day, I really wanted to combine self-care and self-love. That's what sparked my business idea, to help other people coming from where they were, with whatever struggles or obstacles they were facing, to know and understand their worth. Every single person has their own unique gifts and talents, and no matter what they face, they can do anything they set their mind to. I felt that it was very synchronistic.

I didn't know that being a general practitioner would break my heart so much for other women. When people trust in you with their most vulnerable moments and truths, and you hear women who are beautiful, successful, and talented confess that they feel small, worthless and invaluable, it's heartbreaking. You hear them share memories that make them feel shame or loathing; this is not just one woman but many...you realize that every woman has self-doubt, and self-sabotages and that we are our own worst critics. I too have these thoughts, these insecurities – things that most likely no one else is even aware of or notices – that I try to hide about myself.

With Love, Megan is inspired by so many facets; to help other women to step into their power and build their life by design as well as to spark cultivation of a radical self-love journey. I just couldn't wait to share what I had learned with other people. We all have insecurities and we are in turn beautiful, and worthy. It is a lovely thing to know we are not the only ones who have gone through something and to feel like we can relate and grow stronger as a community.

Being in the healthcare industry for most of my life, I wasn't sure where to start in business. In the beginning, I was paralyzed with the need for perfection and lack of business knowledge. I hired a business coach and learned all things tech. I also learned how to create my own website and created my one-to-one course. I am now working on the launch of my six-week transformation course, 'Spark Your Self-Love'.

This business has caused me to completely step outside of my comfort zone. It has challenged me in ways I never thought possible. Where there has been fear, there has also been massive growth and success. Within five short months, my business blossomed. I realized that if I stood in my own way, fearful of sharing my message, putting myself out there and being real and open, I would never get started. I would never make a change and worst of all I would never make an impact.

Since I have stepped out of my own way, I have been able to run fun, free three-day challenges, share a free 'five days of self-love guide', and I have been able to help women all over the world, which is more than I could have ever even hoped for. I have also been invited onto various podcasts as a guest speaker, and I have been invited to speak at live events and conferences within the community. It is so very true that collaboration is greater than competition, and I feel this is only the beginning of my journey.

If it were not for my courage to get over my fears and take this step forward with pursuing my business, I would have never met or collaborated with so many amazing, powerful and talented women across the world or had the opportunity to be a part of the amazing 'She is Unstoppable Movement'. It has been such a fantastic experience. It's also amazing to get feedback, messages, and texts from clients saying how I am making a difference and an impact on their lives. Not to mention it has completely changed mine.

There is nothing so powerful as a woman who believes she is beautiful... worthy.

No matter what that fear may look like for you. Whether it's leaving a toxic relationship (for me divorce), not hiding your body anymore, raising your hand to speak up… that is what self-love and self-worth mean to me. We need to fill ourselves up each day, to be strong, full, and capable of taking each day full on.

My business idea came to me when I stepped into my power. When I had decided enough was enough and that I was going to start loving myself again. Once I had gone through a tremendous amount of my own healing. I knew that I was meant for more, to help others in a bigger capacity, and to share my message and my journey with other women.

Also, having been a nurse for the past eight years and now a nurse practitioner, I had so many ideas about sharing health and wellness, and self-care and self-love. I wanted to integrate the two. It felt like the perfect avenue for me. That's what gave me the idea to become a self-love and development coach.

My current mission in life is to serve women who have been in a similar situation to me, helping women who may not feel good enough or fearful of stepping into their power; who feel like they are worthless, and showing them how much they are truly worth and helping them to live life by their design. I use my knowledge and my past experiences to help others who may have to put themselves on the back-burner, and I teach them self-care techniques and daily rituals and ways to restore self-love into their lives. I am also passionate about helping to serve the poor and vulnerable within the community.

I want to say to any woman reading this right now, who may have gone through something similar to me, that first of all, do not ever try to convince yourself that you deserve to be treated in any way less than the queen that you are, or that you did something wrong. Because you didn't.

If you are ever in an unsafe situation, make a safe plan for yourself. If you do not feel safe, tell someone and get out.

YOU ARE STRONG ENOUGH.

You are brilliant, capable, powerful and beautiful – do what is needed for you.

Do not care what anyone else will think about you or your situation — the only person that matters at this moment is you.

If you feel like you can't cope, you shouldn't suffer in silence.

You are not a failure if something in your life doesn't always go as planned – this is a learning experience. Remember, we are always failing forward. When one door closes, just know that God has a better door waiting for you.

Let things go. Don't hold onto the hurt, the bitterness, the resentment, the sadness. Just forgive. 'Bless and Release'. It's part of my morning routine, and I could not be happier now. Give yourself time to heal – but do not be too hard on yourself. Try your best, live life each and every day. Do not live in the past.

This is truly what inspired my business mission, to overcome your fears, and to design a life that you love... because you only get one life. So, make it beautiful and the best one you can possibly imagine. We are not guaranteed tomorrow. We only have this moment, so don't waste it wishing, regretting, being fearful; or worst of all, not being happy wishing you had done something that you were too scared to do.

No woman... In fact, no person should ever be made to feel worthless or less than incredible. I believe every relationship has two sides and we should treat each other as we wish to be treated. We all deserve to be treated incredibly.

We all have amazing qualities, we all have unique gifts, and we all have a purpose.

We are all extraordinary.

No matter how many people try to tear us down, no matter what anyone says, it is imperative that: WE HOLD THAT IN OUR HEARTS AND BELIEVE THAT ABOUT OURSELVES.

Let your light shine, do what is true in your heart and be a woman determined to rise.

ABOUT THE AUTHOR

Megan is a self-love and development coach and founder of With Love, Megan, a platform dedicated to empowering, inspiring and supporting women to overcome their fears and design a life they love. Megan is on a mission to help women learn to love their true authentic selves, realizing and understanding their self-worth. As a coach Megan brings her infectious, positive and uplifting energy to her clients.

Megan is also a family nurse practitioner with eight years prior RN experience. She works within the community to promote preventative health and wellness to individuals of all ages. Megan earned degrees in a Master of Science in Nursing from Gonzaga University and a Bachelor of Science in Nursing from Walla Walla University.

Megan has participated in several international mission trips helping the vulnerable and under-served population by participating in various health clinics and also by building needed homes throughout their communities. She also volunteers for the Make a Wish Foundation. Megan is actively involved in spreading self-love inspiration and education in online communities. From speaking at live events to being featured in podcasts and live videos, Megan is always looking for new opportunities to empower women to step into their most confident selves.

MEGAN FRASIER

Self-love and development coach and founder of With Love, Megan.
www.withlovemegan.com

 Self Love Junkie Tribe (private group)

 @withlove_megan

"Your perfect imperfection is perfect to me!"

– Jennifer Hardie

Joanna Petrie-Rout

walked away from my old role in December, and in February, a few weeks later, I started back with this group of people who I loved working with.

And then something bizarre happened. All of my friends and family were really desperate for me to find somebody and be happy; they'd encouraged me to start internet dating, and it was something I just really didn't connect with. I didn't want to do it. I found it clinical. However, I went along with it to keep people happy. In mid-February, I received an email notification to say my membership for this online dating company had auto-renewed, and I can remember feeling really frustrated because I was thinking, 'I just don't like it, I don't enjoy it, and now I've just paid for another six months of it.' I decided to have a little word with myself and see it as an opportunity. I decided to revamp my profile. I wrote a poem about my personality, and I put it onto the system and didn't really think anything more.

The very next day, Rob sent me a message, and over the following week, we exchanged lots of emails, texts and phone calls. We then decided we would meet on the Saturday. This was just not like me at all! We agreed to meet in a pub car park. At the time, we were living about 180 miles away from each other, and we decided we'd meet half-way. It wasn't like we were just meeting around the corner, we had to make quite a concerted effort to get there. I can remember pulling up in the carpark, getting out, seeing Rob and him walking across that car park to meet me. He literally grabbed my hand, and I remember just looking at him and knowing I'd found my soulmate.

I never believed in fairy tales, but my dad always said to me, 'You're going to meet somebody and you're going to know. You're just going to know, and you're going to be swept off your feet.' I never really believed it but what was so special is I knew Rob felt exactly the same. He held my hand, and we kissed. We've been inseparable ever since. My internet date turned out to be my fairytale, which I can assure you, I didn't think it would be.

Rob was living in the Lake District, and I was living in Cheshire and working in Birmingham during the week. I would get back to Cheshire on a Friday, unpack my case, repack my case, and then go and spend pretty much every weekend in the Lake District with him. It was lovely. We spent a lot of time thinking about our future and we both had the same kind of ambitions. It was just beautiful, and within thirteen months, we got married in the Lake District. It was the whirlwind I never thought would happen, and it was just incredible. Rob literally is my life.

It was like I'd had a universal intervention, because if I hadn't made the decision in December to walk away from my job, I wouldn't have been able to make the relationship with Rob work. I think it would have turned out completely differently. My instinct was to try and fight it out, to battle through. I would never have given up that job on my own. I firmly believe the Universe was saying to me, 'Do you know what? You've got to do something different, and you're never going to get there on your own terms, so I'm going to intervene and do something for you.'

We decided straight away that we wanted to start a family. We were both forty and recognised that time wasn't on our side. We'd both wanted to have children, but the paths we'd gone down just hadn't enabled that to happen. I had desperately wanted to be a mum but because of my personal circumstances, I think I suppressed it. So, to suddenly find myself in a situation where I was marrying the man of my dreams, my soulmate, and trying for a family, felt like a dream had come true for me.

Here I was in the beautiful Lake District. Rob had changed career a few years before. He'd got to a point where he felt like he wasn't making a difference so made a change. He retrained as a teacher, and when I saw him talk about the difference he was making to his students' lives, his eyes would literally light up. One day we had a conversation about what I was doing, and he'd said to me, 'Look, I get the impression that you've fallen a little bit out of love with what you were doing.'

The truth was, having spent most of my career in personal development and helping people in the corporate world to become the best they can be and to uncover their talent and potential, I had fallen out of love with my own. I didn't have the same pleasure for it anymore. He said to me, 'Why don't you take a year off while you're up here, concentrate on your health, and your wellbeing and we'll concentrate on trying to have a family. You can then give yourself the time to really think about what would make your eyes light up and what you could do next.'

So that's what we did, and it was the first real period in my life where I hadn't been working. I went from an environment where I'd been working with friends and being busy, to a situation where I didn't know anybody and had lots of time on my hands. Rob worked long hours. He would go out of the house early in the morning, and wouldn't get back until late at night. I was sat focusing on the fact that we were trying to get pregnant, but it wasn't happening, and I didn't know what my next step was going to be. I just didn't know how I was going to continue to contribute and make a difference in the world. I think over a period of a few months, I felt like I slowly got more and more isolated and I started to lose the sense of who I was and what my purpose was.

I actually became quite insecure, lonely, and depressed, which is not my natural state. I'm usually very bubbly, and confident, but I just reached a point where I couldn't see the positive in anything. I felt so frustrated, and one day, when I felt like I just couldn't take that anymore, I started to look online for jobs. I think the Universe worked its little miracle again because, on the day I looked, I suddenly found that there was a role for a leadership development consultant being advertised locally, about forty minutes from home. I applied for it and got it. After having had eleven months off, sitting at home, trying to discover what my purpose was and trying to achieve my ambition of being a mum, I gave up and went back to doing what I was good at, so I could at least build up my confidence again. I settled into the job, and we continued to try for a family, but it just wasn't happening. Every month we ended up really disappointed. We decided that we needed some help and to talk to the doctors about receiving some fertility treatment.

We started to go through a barrage of tests. It felt like every week, one of us was at the hospital or doctors for another test. All we kept hearing back was that there was no explanation for our infertility and that we should just keep trying. All around me, I kept seeing people sharing happy news about the fact that they were pregnant. I tried so hard to be happy for them, but it began to get more and more difficult. I started to feel resentful, which is not a quality I enjoy. In the summer of 2014, we decided we would go through IVF. We were so hopeful, but I have to be honest, I didn't realise how tough the process is, both physically and emotionally. Living in West Cumbria made it more challenging as it's such a remote area, you can't access some of the treatment locally.

To get the treatment we needed, we had to travel to the nearest hospital in Manchester. We decided we were prepared to do that, and so as we started to gear up to have IVF, I would get up at the crack of dawn and drive two and a half hours down to Manchester, literally to have a blood test, and then turn round again and drive two and a half hours back just to go to work. At a time when you're advised to try and keep stress to a minimum, and to really look after yourself, I was doing something that was really quite exhausting. We did it because we believed it would be worth it to have a baby and to fulfil our dream.

In the July of 2014, we had the IVF, and then in August, we learned it hadn't worked. I remember me and Rob were sat on the bed holding each other and crying. I honestly, don't think we ever really talked much more about it after that. I think we kept hoping it would happen but we decided we wouldn't go through IVF again because of our ages and other factors. It felt like it was best that we just slowly got on with our lives. It was devastating.

When you go through IVF, there are so many chemicals and hormones put into your body. I think it left me feeling quite emotionally wrung out.

Then in October of that year, my dad passed away in his sleep. I honestly believe that my dad waited around until he knew both of his girls were settled and happy. I think he gave up without my mum around anymore. My dad had been everything to me, and I was so, so pleased we'd managed to spend all that time together when Mum had been ill and after Mum had passed. I think it made it just that little bit more bearable to cope with. I felt like the colour literally drained out of my life that year. I was battered emotionally and physically from having to deal with the failed IVF and then had to deal with the loss of my dad. I became the shadow of my former self.

At the time, Rob's career was beginning to go from strength to strength. After retraining and becoming a newly qualified teacher a few years before, he went on to become a deputy head at a local school. He then became the headteacher. I was so proud of him and happy to be his wife. And yet, while I was delighted for him, seeing his life and his career take off, I literally felt like I was living the same day every day. I was still doing the same corporate job. A job I could do with my eyes closed. It was comfortable, but it certainly wasn't stretching or challenging me. I remember sitting at my desk one day, and I thought, 'Look, you've only got fifteen years left working, so you can do this. Just suck it up and get on with it.'

When I reflect on that now, I know that's what drives me to help the women I support. I don't want anyone to feel like that. I don't want anyone to believe their circumstances mean they have to settle. I think we all have something extraordinary in us. We can achieve so much. It's just about getting clear about what's going to light your soul and taking courageous steps in that direction.

I'm naturally a positive person and don't like having a negative mindset. I decided I was going to take up running and joined a running club with my friend Claire. I'm not a natural runner. I'm not built for it, but I decided that's what I was going to do. We started to do the couch to 5k programme. I actually found myself enjoying it. Claire and I slowly got better at running, and we were soon running two to three times a week. I felt like I got physically and mentally stronger.

It was an excellent way of escaping the constant frustration of not feeling like I was either living my purpose, contributing in a meaningful way, or achieving my goal to be a mum. I was still clinging on to the hope that we'd get a miracle. Then, one afternoon Rob and I started watching a programme about the Coast to Coast Walk, which is very close to the Cumbrian Hearts. It was created by the Cumbrian writer, Alfred Wainwright, and starts in St Bees in Cumbria. It's basically a 192-mile walk from one side of the country to the other. You start on the West coast by dipping your boots in the sea and pick up a pebble. You walk 192 miles and throw your pebble in the sea on the other side of the country as you dip your boots back into the water at Robin Hood's Bay. It takes you through three National Parks and covers some of the most incredible scenery in the UK. So, it's a challenge for sure.

I don't know how it happened, but I suddenly found myself convincing Rob that that was how we should spend our summer holiday. We both enjoyed walking, but we had never really tackled anything as big as the Coast to Coast. We decided to follow the itinerary laid out in the Wainwright book, which basically gets you to do the walk over twelve days, covering seventeen to eighteen miles on average a day. Before we could change our minds, I booked the trip for July 2016. At the same time, I agreed to run my first half marathon with Claire in support of Parkinson's. I trained hard during the week and then on the weekends, Rob and I went out walking in preparation for the Coast to Coast. I was getting fit and strong, but I think I was trying to block out some of the feelings bubbling away. I guess I was pushing the sadness about my mum and dad to one side, but the exercise was really doing me good. You won't be surprised to hear, I pushed myself too hard again, and I developed a condition in my foot called Plantar Fasciitis. It's a really painful condition that affects the ligament running underneath the sole of your foot. At its worst, you can't put your heel on the floor. At a time when I was trying to train for a walk of 192 miles and a thirteen-mile run, it wasn't ideal, but I just kept on going.

I remember questioning whether I could actually do it because I was in so much pain. As you'll tell from my story, there's a theme here about really not wanting to quit. I think it was the 25th of July when Rob and I put on our backpacks, dipped our boots in the water and set off across the UK. The Coast to Coast was one of the most life-changing experiences of my life. I believe it was the catalyst for why I'm doing what I do now. Along the route, you meet people from all over the world. You take on the challenge together. There's such a beautiful feeling of connectedness. You sometimes see the same faces day in and day out, or you just see people taking their time on it.

Rob and I soon got into a routine. We'd get up in the morning, start walking, and push as far as we could before we sat and had lunch. We'd feel exhausted but really exhilarated as we arrived in a little village where we'd be staying for the night. Every night was pretty much the same. It was a quick shower, write up a journal for the day, so we didn't forget the experience, and then we'd grab something to eat, and get some rest. My foot wasn't getting any better, so every morning I would get up, and not be able to put my foot on the floor. It would take about half an hour to ease into it. I'd get my boots on, and start walking, but as the day went on, I began to really limp.

On day five we got to a village where we limped into it literally, and when I took off my boot, I discovered I had an incredibly massive blister on the side of my ankle. I really didn't know what to do for the best. The minute I took my boot off, my foot started to swell. Overnight it became so painful. I wasn't sure I was actually going to get my boot on the next day, but I did. So, I managed to get some blister plasters, strap my foot up, and get back on with it. Over the next few days, that's what we did, but things got progressively worse.

There were days where I would have to take painkillers just to be able to get my foot on the floor. There was one morning in particular where I hadn't slept because I'd been in so much pain. I woke up and laid in Rob's arms crying with how much pain I was in. I think we were about three days from the end, and Rob just held me close and whispered to me that we could call it a day if I wanted to. I just couldn't do that. Rob was so supportive and encouraging, and gave me the time to get my head together. We took our time getting ready. I squeezed my foot into my boot, took the painkillers, and limped off.

When you're walking something like the Coast to Coast, you get a lot of time to think and to go inside your head as you put one foot in front of the other. I spent a lot of time thinking about where I was in my life, the things that had happened, what was important to me, and some of the challenges I had faced. I started to face the reality of what I had metaphorically and physically been running away from.

On the last night of our walk, as we sat in the hotel room, I opened up to Rob about my feelings. I remember sitting on the bed crying and saying to him, 'I have got to say this. I have got to be able to get this out...it's time to give up on the dream of becoming parents, Rob. It's time for me to find a new dream.'

It took a lot for me to get to that point because I'm endlessly hopeful, but I knew I couldn't keep doing it to myself. I knew that life is too short, that I was settling, and I wasn't making the impact I wanted to make. I had a great sense of purpose, and I just needed to find it. Rob gave me a cuddle, and we had a cry.

On the last night of that walk, we let the dream go.

The next day I literally crawled into Robin Hood's Bay. I dipped my boots in the sea, and we threw our little pebbles from St Bees into the ocean. I sat there thinking, 'my God, that walk has nearly broken me', but I also knew that walk had just saved me because I was in such a different mindset. I was in absolute agony, but I was in a different mindset. I don't think I even realised at the time how much of a life-changing experience that walk would be for me.

When I got home, I started thinking differently about what I was going to do. Even though I was still in pain with my heel, I managed to run the Great North Run with Claire. It was very slow and painful, but we did it. I started to research and do some thinking about the kind of things that really lit me up and ways I could make a difference if I were to follow a different path. Every time I thought about it, I kept coming back to the word: service. I have always loved helping make a difference to people's lives, whether it's been in the corporate roles that I've done, through my friendships and family, or through the coaching I've done. It's what has motivated me throughout my life.

Over those past few years I lost my faith in the Law of Attraction. I really disconnected from it, and I felt it was time to embrace it again. I started to re-read information about it, practiced the principles, and got back in alignment with my spiritual beliefs. In doing that, I came across an exercise. There was a list of five things, and it asked you to pick two to set an intention around using the Law of Attraction. I chose to receive an unexpected gift and to hear from a friend I'd not heard from in a long time.

Literally, within a couple of hours, I received a text from an American friend of mine, Tammy, who I hadn't heard from in months. She had been part of an online group of women in their forties who were trying to conceive. Because she'd been successful, I don't think she wanted to rub my face in it, so we hadn't stayed in close contact. Out of the blue, on the day I decided to do this, she texted me and said I'm often in her thoughts. It was beautiful and lovely to hear from her and to let her know I was moving on with my life. I was astonished at the synchronicity of that message. Then that same night, Rob came home from work, and he'd bought me an unexpected present that I was absolutely stunned by. I had set these two intentions on the same day, and both of them came true!

I knew this was the Law of Attraction in action.

Little did I know at the time, but the present he'd bought me was going to be another significant part of my transformation. The gift was Jo Malone's autobiography. Rob knew I liked Jo Malone. I just hadn't appreciated how transformative the book was going to be and what an impact her personal story would have on me. I don't know if you've read it, but the book is beautiful. It was a hardback book, and on the front cover there was a scented page. The scent was the perfume she created when she moved away from Jo Malone and created her second brand. The smell was Pomelo. It's such a beautiful, fresh and uplifting fragrance. Every time I picked up the book to read it, I could just breathe that smell in.

I read the book quickly and devoured everything she said. Jo Malone is somebody who has not always had it easy but has an enduring spirit. I felt really emotionally connected to her resilience and passion. We certainly haven't had the same path, but certain things in her story really resonated with me.

The book inspired me so much that when I got to the last page, I sat back, and I just knew it was going to be the catalyst for making dramatic changes in my life. I started to draw on all of the tools I've used with all of the coaching and corporate clients I've worked with. I began to personally apply all the techniques I have used with others to help them discover their potential. I really didn't limit myself in any way. I started to go wacky and explored crazy ideas about what my next step would be. I really started to become energised again.

I began to discover that I have an entrepreneurial spirit I never even knew existed. My creativity and my ambition fired up, and I started to feel completely different. What struck me though, was that after all the soul-searching I had done over the previous years of trying to find my path and my purpose, I kept coming back to the principle of 'you're here to serve and help others', which isn't dramatically different to what I did in my corporate career. The opportunity now was about taking it in a different direction where I could have a more significant impact.

I realised I wasn't the only woman who reaches her mid-life and gets that feeling that there has to be more. I knew my journey wasn't unique. I knew it wasn't right for me to help other people to find their purpose after infertility, because I felt it was too raw. I knew it was broader than that. I knew women were questioning what comes next for them. Women who had reached a crossroads in life and knew in their soul they had more to give. The more I started to explore it, the more I realised there are so many women with the same story as me, and I could help them to shortcut the soul-searching because I've been through that. I really wanted to help women who felt lost to rediscover who they are, to dare to dream, to be more, to do more, and have more. That's the path I started to go down.

In 2017 the Universe started to play a hand for me, and a couple of strange things happened. I'd been working hard in my spare time to come up with a name for my coaching business. There was a quote I kept seeing that really resonated with me.

'The right time is always now.'

It was just such a source of inspiration. I didn't really know at the time why it resonated so much, but it just did. I had it displayed everywhere. I was still trying to hone the exact message for my coaching business. I just kept coming back to women moving beyond ordinary to lead extraordinary lives, breaking free from feeling stuck and moving into something that feels remarkable for them.

I still remember the exact moment the name of my business came to me. It was the moment when 'No Ordinary Woman' was born. I was sat in my home office and I'd been looking at that quote and thinking, the right time is always now. The word 'now' kept sticking out to me. It just literally jumped off the page, and then I saw, 'No ordinary woman'. And that was it. That was the moment when everything fell into place for me. One of the funny things is that the Jo Malone scent, Pomelo, has become the smell of my business. I wear the perfume when I'm working on No Ordinary Woman, and I have the candle in my office.

I don't believe there's such a thing as an ordinary woman. I think everybody has something incredible about them, but I think we allow ourselves to get shut down, trapped into situations, and we just don't know the path to follow, or can't see the way. That's what drives me. It's helping women to get that clarity and to know that there's so much more about them.

When I decided that No Ordinary Woman was it, I was still working my corporate job, but my contract was due to end. I made the decision to walk away from corporate and to go full-time in my business. It was scary, but I knew it was what I wanted to do.

Another set of strange circumstances started to unfold. My boss suddenly left the organisation which left the Head of Leadership role vacant, a role I had done many times before. A new HR director joined the business, and I suddenly found myself in the position of being asked to step back into a leadership role within the organisation and extend my contract.

I remember feeling conflicted because on the one hand I was delighted to be given the opportunity to operate at a leadership level in the organisation, but on the other, I felt I was compromising myself because I had made the decision to go off and be an entrepreneur. As I started to establish No Ordinary Woman, I suddenly found I was also becoming really re-energised by the work I was doing in my corporate role.

I think because I'd been asked to step back into a leadership role and had started having an impact and making a difference there, it reignited my passion for leadership development. I managed to negotiate to work part-time hours, which gave me the best of both worlds. Life felt good again. I was doing my corporate job helping leaders reach their potential, and I was building a business supporting women to achieve their potential too.

I don't think I will ever cease to be amazed by some of the synchronicities that get presented to us in life. I was really excited at the development of my own business, but I found I was struggling to sleep because I was so excited by the concept of No Ordinary Woman and what I was doing. I would go to bed, and my brain wouldn't switch off because it was just ticking over with creative ideas.

At the time, someone gifted me a bottle of an essential oil called Serenity, which was supposed to help you relax and unwind. I've got to be honest, I was quite skeptical because, for me, essential oils have always been about making your home smell lovely or what you include in a nice massage, it wasn't about having something plant-based that could help improve your overall health and emotional well-being. I decided I had nothing to lose, and I gave it a go. I was absolutely blown away by the results.

This little bottle of oil helped me quiet my mind, and to relax and unwind at night.

I began to explore some of the other oils. Then I shared them with friends and family and started to see improvements in their health and wellbeing too, resolving health issues they'd struggled with for years. I loved that I had finally found something that was natural and could support so many health and wellbeing challenges in such a pure and beautiful way.

I was given the opportunity to become an advocate for DoTerra. I decided to take the chance, although it wasn't something I had ever thought I'd be involved in. Over the next few months, I started to realise how powerful the blend of mindset, wellbeing, and spiritual practice had been in transforming my life. I had blended mindset techniques and tools, used essential oils, and committed to a daily spiritual practice to get me to the point that I was at. I really wanted to give other women the opportunity to combine these transformative approaches so they could achieve their aspirations too. So, that's what shaped the business philosophy I have today.

Each day I wake up and use these tools in my life to help me accomplish the things I want to achieve. When I do this my life unfolds beautifully. I start my day with being grateful and getting myself into a high vibe mindset. The essential oils help me overcome any emotional or health challenges I'm feeling. I spend half an hour every morning journalling and experiencing the benefits of meditation to help me connect with something bigger than myself.

That's the gift I bring to the women I work with, to help them understand the power of mastering their mind, body, and soul. I've gone from feeling lost, lonely, and desperate, to waking up each day knowing that I am aligned to my purpose, that I have all the tools I need to ensure I get the most from every day.

I feel like I've had a very blessed and happy life. One of my favourite authors, Gabby Bernstein says, 'Obstacles are detours in the right direction'. I honestly believe that the last seven years were just bumps in the road that edged me in the direction of stepping into my true purpose. Becoming a mother wasn't part of my journey, but it has been the catalyst for so many beautiful moments. If I had become a mother, I wouldn't be following the path I'm on now. I wouldn't be able to support other women to move beyond what I call the ordinary, and to step into their brilliance.

For me, that's everything...absolutely everything.

When I see a woman standing at that crossroads, getting frustrated because she doesn't know the path to take and feeling like she should just stay there, I literally hear my heart whisper....

I see you, I know you, I was you, and I can help you.

ABOUT THE AUTHOR

Joanna Petrie-Rout is a mentor and transformation coach to women who are tired of settling and who are ready to be more, do more and have more. Her mission is simple: to help women globally to break free from their limitations and step in to their brilliance.

In 2016, feeling lost and disillusioned with her corporate career and slowly coming to terms with her own infertility, Joanna completed a 200-mile trek across England. It was the catalyst for a period of dramatic personal transformation. She was physically and mentally challenged and came to realise that she could achieve more than she thought possible and had allowed herself to play small.

Joanna became the founder of 'No Ordinary Woman' and now mentors women to discover their true desires, bust through their blocks, take bold action and achieve the transformation required to live an extraordinary life. Her approach is unique as she blends a combination of mindset work, essential oils and spiritual practice to achieve incredible results for her clients.

Her new programme 'Limitless' launches in January.

Joanna is married to her soulmate Rob, has two gorgeous cats and is blessed to live an extraordinary life every day.

JOANNA PETRIE-ROUT

Mentor and transformation coach.
www.no-ordinary-woman.com

 @NOWtribe

 @iamnoordinarywoman

"Too often we underestimate the power of a touch, a smile, a kind word, a listening ear, an honest compliment, or the smallest act of caring, all of which have the potential to turn a life around."

– Leo Buscaglia

Cassandra Queeley

CHAPTER 8
A path less travelled...the journey to my authentic self.
By Cassandra Queeley

"There is no limit to what we, as women, can accomplish."
– Michelle Obama

Right now, I'm in the middle of a business rebirth and rebrand. I used to think I had to have a plan for everything (you know the one...make sure all of the i's are dotted, and the t's are crossed) and that changing my mind on my business direction every day meant I didn't have it together.

But the reality is, change is inevitable. It's totally natural and incredible to be in my current phase of growth and up-levelling.

At the moment, I'm creating a brand-new website which is aligned to me and my personality. It's also helping me to strengthen my skills and provide an even better service for my incredible clients.

My business is growing fast, but it hasn't been easy. I didn't have a clue how it would evolve, and you don't have to either!

The most important thing is to get started.

I've gone from being a virtual assistant, helping out entrepreneurs in general, to working with some of the most incredible female entrepreneurs around the globe. I couldn't be more excited!

It's amazing what can happen when you choose to trust in yourself and the direction the universe pulls you in!

OK...I'm getting way ahead of myself here. I've been talking to you for like a minute and I haven't even introduced myself, where are my manners? *clears throat* Hello there....my name is Cassandra Queeley and I'm an Entrepreneur Support Specialist, here to assist you in all things virtual assistance so that you can scale and lead your business to the top, where it belongs! It's a pleasure to meet you (through these pages at least) ... Did you like my little elevator pitch there? Not bad is it? Got you thinking, didn't I? Well, it wasn't always like that. I didn't always have the words to engage and connect.

Let me take you back a little. I started my business a couple of years ago when I was made redundant. I used to be the PA to the CEO of a global company. I loved working there and thought that I'd be there for years. So, I was devastated when they let me go. The thought of not seeing the people I had worked with and built relationships with (inside and outside the office) was a tough one to handle. It took time to process, and I'm not embarrassed to say, there were a few tears shed (especially during the conversation in the meeting room...talk about awkward!). I can laugh now, but back then, oh boy, it was as painful as having a tooth pulled out without any anaesthetic! Not to mention, I was also going through a personal crisis at the time too.

When it rains...it pours!

I was also constantly poked, prodded and tested for an illness the doctors and specialists were unable to diagnose. It added stress on my life, and I was depressed for a while. The stress of not knowing why I was in constant pain and unable to do simple tasks without great difficulty (like walk) took its toll. It really sucked because on the outside I looked perfectly fine, but on the inside, I felt like a train had just run me over then doubled back to run me over again for good measure!

With all of that going on, I was 'in my head' a lot. Thinking about my life, internalising the pain, struggling to keep up my usual happy and positive outlook. It was non-stop! But it did make me realise that losing my job was probably the best thing that had happened to me.

I'm a firm believer in 'things happen for a reason'.

It made me focus on my physical and mental health and make the decision to find a way of making money that would enable me to manage my illness while working from home. I knew I had a lot to offer and I didn't necessarily want to do that working for a big corporation. Nor could I, since I was potentially an unreliable candidate for employment. I was barely able to get out of bed in the morning, let alone commute to work and be a stellar employee on a daily basis. I decided that I wanted to still do what I do, but do it my way.

That very attitude is what led me to set up my own company. The day I decided to do that was on the 8th of March, which is International Women's Day. Feeling empowered and inspired I thought about what I wanted for my life, which then led me to decide to use my skills and experience and come from a place of service...and so it all began to take shape.

As a PA, I had attended a number of industry events, so I was already aware of the term Virtual Assistant and what they do. It made sense to go down that road. What I didn't know at the time was that you can be a VA providing services to all kinds of industries and niches. I started to think about what types of businesses I wanted to support. I was still living in Luxembourg at the time. I moved there in 2005 to provide a better life for my son and me. The country was going through a major push for start-ups, ventures, and innovation companies at the time, and I decided to reach out to them to offer my services.

It didn't go so well...firstly, no one knew what a VA is or does so I was having to explain the concept over and over again, and secondly, because they were unfamiliar, they were reluctant to hire me. They didn't understand the whole 'virtual' thing. I spent most of my time explaining that I wasn't a temp and I wouldn't be situated in their office.

It was exhausting. Like a speed date from hell!

I did manage to find a couple of clients but that didn't stop me from feeling like a failure and disheartened, especially as networking isn't my forte and I had to muster up all of my energy to hide away my shyness.

That all took its toll on me and my health started to deteriorate even further, so I decided to put my business on hold and focus on finding out what my prognosis was, and if there was a way to manage or cure my illness.

It took almost three years and a lot of tests and medicine to find that I probably have Lupus! A chronic and incurable auto-immune disease where the body's immune system becomes hyperactive and attacks healthy tissue, so basically my body is attacking itself.

Even though it wasn't a definitive diagnosis, it did give me a sense of relief and helped me to rebuild my mindset and start to manage my illness and my life too. I started from then to rebuild myself, and with the help of some medication and a mindset shift, I began to feel like I could manage my illness and live the life I wanted. I started to listen more to my body, and to shape my life and rebuild my business around my health. Which is what led me to rethink how I wanted to run my business, who I wanted to work with and how I could create a life that included my passion for travel.

I have always travelled. I love seeing new places, meeting new people, and experiencing different cultures. Travel has been a part of my life from as far back as I can remember. Becoming a Digital Nomad made sense for me. It was a natural progression. I'd already been to forty-four countries, before I even knew what a Digital Nomad was!

A Digital Nomad is a person who has no fixed abode, someone that travels, and lives and works in different places. They either have their own business or work for a company that lets them be location-independent.

They have the freedom to work from anywhere!

One of the strengths I wholeheartedly embrace, is my ability to plan. So even though I knew I wanted to live a location-independent life, I needed to know how it was going to work. I did my research, read blogs, chatted to other DNs online and mapped out the things I needed to do to make it happen. I put together a twelve-month plan consisting of tasks like selling my apartment, getting rid of old clothes, and boxing up and putting my personal items into storage.

It all pretty much went to plan. Never underestimate the power of a good plan. It helps you focus, stay motivated, and sets you on the path to enlightenment (okay...maybe not the last one but it does help clear your mind!).

I started my travels in June 2018 in Japan. The first destination was non-negotiable for me. I've always wanted to visit Japan - cut to the misspent youth of me watching Manga movies and wanting to be in the TV show Shogun!

That was the birth of my digital nomad life. I decided to spend a month touring Japan. Having the freedom to do so without restraint was exhilarating.

I was in charge of my life and living it my way.

I knew that I was going to enjoy visiting Japan, but wow, I wasn't prepared for the feeling I had the moment I arrived. I absolutely loved the place and immediately started to see myself living there.

It was love at first sight...especially when I spotted the Hello Kitty shop.

The place is so vibrant, different, and exciting. The food is great, and the people are amazing. But I think what made me love it even more, was the fact I was free to be me. I could roam around the streets and feel safe and feel good. And, despite it being a hugely busy and overpopulated place, I felt at ease and comfortable, which was surprising because, even though I'm from the city of Manchester, I'm not really a city girl. I'm not into the hustle and bustle, you know? But there I was, going with the flow and fitting in like a local.

I generally try to embrace life fully, especially when it comes to travel. I'm not scared to travel alone, but for a fleeting moment, while I was on the plane heading there, I freaked out a little and asked myself if I was doing the right thing. The slight panic of 'what have I done?' crept in. Thankfully, it only lasted a moment. I knew in my heart it was right for me, and my worries and apprehensions quickly dispelled. (Take that! You pesky imposter syndrome...not today!).

I was mindful that I still had a business to run, so I made sure that I could still work and be a tourist too. My experiences of travelling around Japan, meeting locals and expats, being fitted for and wearing a kimono, being interviewed for a Japanese TV show, staying in a Pod (like sleeping in an MRI machine) and Capsule (not like sleeping in an MRI machine) hotel, learning how to write my name in Japanese at a personal calligraphy class, visiting the Cup Noodle Museum, donning a Shogun outfit (high five from my ten-year-old self!), visiting Disney and Universal and basically having an absolute blast, all while building my business, reaffirmed that this was the life for me.

This life is amazing, and sure...I'm 'living the dream' but don't let my Facebook posts and check-ins fool you. This life isn't for everyone. It can be tough. Life, in general, can be tough, so this is no different.

I have a tendency to live in the now. It's what drives me and keeps me going through this crazy thing called life. I sometimes neglect to look back on what I've achieved with gratitude and appreciation. I rarely stop to think, 'How the hell did I get here?' I find that's something we as women do a lot. We are usually taught to do what needs to be done, not to complain, and accept our roles and carry on. If we do something, anything that resembles greatness, we merely get a cursory pat on the head. We are told to not let it go to our heads and move on.

Do what we are supposed to do.

I used to think that I wasn't 'one of those' women. I'm strong-willed, I go against the grain, and I'm a bit of a rebel. So, no way was I going to get caught up in all that!

I went to a progressive school, and my aunts are badass role models, dammit! Oh, how wrong I was. While I wasn't looking, insecurities, self-loathing, uncertainty, and doubt, all crept in through the back door, kicked off their shoes and made themselves comfortable. Years of having my every decision challenged, defending myself after someone had decided to force their judgement upon me, trying to be heard over the din of denials took a toll that I didn't even realise I was paying. All of those times that I bit back and struck a blow to a judgmental ego, karate-chopped a snarky comment, I thought I was winning. That my strength, self-belief, and actions were shielding me from harm. Little did I know that seeds of negativity were being planted in my psyche.

Something needed to be done.

Breaking a habit is not so easy. Finding my true self is a journey and a path less travelled by me. I'm working on it at the moment. I write in my 5-minute journal every day, meditate, have guilt-free 'me' time and I'll continue doing more in my pursuit of happiness. However, in spite of all of the negativity that sometimes shrouds me, I'm thankful for every day that I'm able to do this, and I'm also proud that I created this life for myself too. When I look back on my life and all that's happened, and everything that's led me to this point, I am finally beginning to acknowledge how far I have come. It's taken time to be able to praise myself for my achievements but I'm getting there slowly.

How far have I come, you ask? Well...grab a seat and let me take you back to the start of my journey.

I was an inquisitive kid. Mature for my age. I always wanted to know things, so I read a lot and tried to absorb everything around me. I was pretty strong-willed, didn't have a problem voicing my opinions and always stood up for the underdog...I still do. I have a talent for being able to intuitively understand a person's plight, feel their upset, pain, or joy, and be the support they need. The urge to help and support people has always been within me. I was probably an empath in the making. The need to be there for everyone and make sure that they're happy, regardless of how I was feeling, was strong and still is if I'm honest.

My thirst for knowledge first and foremost and the confidence that inevitably comes with that, didn't always go down so well. I was branded a know-it-all, and it rubbed some people up the wrong way. Children and adults alike. It was one of those 'stuck between a rock and a hard place' situations where people would take advantage and get advice, opinions, and information from me, but the moment they didn't like what I had to say...well you can guess the rest! I was such a happy-go-lucky person that I tried to not let it affect me. I embraced the fact that I liked to know things and if I didn't or I was wrong, that was cool because it meant I would either learn the right way or find out something new.

I was also the kid with all of her fingers in all of the pies. Involved in everything at school. School was such a happy place for me. I loved it! Both Primary and Secondary school are at the top of my list of things that I would like to relive. I was in the netball, basketball and football teams. I was musically talented, so I played the piano, the violin, viola, guitar, Russian instruments, you name it...I tried to play it. I also sang in the choir and had my hand up volunteering for everything that took my fancy. I don't know how I had the time or energy to do it all (oh to be young again).

I loved every minute of it and to be honest, my home life sucked. I was unhappy, so I decided to create my own happiness. It paid off because I had a blast. I was being my authentic self, doing the things I loved. But yet again that garnered negative reactions. 'Who does she think she is?' (I was just being me), 'She's pretending to be posh' (I was the second chair in the South Manchester Orchestra, can't I be proud?), 'She's so stuck up and thinks she's better than us' (umm, say what now?). This all seemed crazy to me.

Once I took a step back, I got it. I was an inner-city kid, living in one of the most gang-riddled areas in Manchester and here's me bleating on about how much I love the arts and how going to the theatre, art galleries and museums were my jam. It wasn't really the thing to do when you were from 'The Hood'.

I was in concerts with the South Manchester Orchestra as a violist, travelling the country in a Russian ensemble (I played the Balalaika and Domra and sang in Russian), I went to Russia twice, saw original paintings from the likes of Picasso, Gauguin, Rembrandt, and Van Gogh, put flowers on the graves of Dostoevsky and Tchaikovsky and performed at the Royal Albert Hall. All before I was sixteen!

I was experiencing something that not many inner-city kids got to experience and although I was young, I was fully aware of the magnitude of it all and was extremely grateful and appreciative.

I was different.

I've always known that, and so did they. But what some failed to see was that I was also the same as them. I hung out with friends, listened to the same music, liked the same boys, and plonked myself front and center of the TV whenever a cool show was on (shout out to Knightrider, The A-Team, and MacGyver).

I just so happened to also like other things that they didn't. I embraced it all. I was an all-rounder, enjoying and exploring every aspect of my personality. And because of that, I made a conscious decision to make friends based on my interests. It worked out pretty well: I got to enjoy my interests with like-minded people and was able to connect with pretty much everyone I met.

My teenage years were quite diverse and filled with interactions that I probably wouldn't have had if I hadn't decided to embrace all of me (quirks and all). That adeptness came in handy as an adult too. My interpersonal skills rock!

Doing a gazillion activities started to take its toll though. I was never a straight A student, but I was usually above average. Cut to the end of Secondary school where I came out with hardly any GCSEs. Bugger! In hindsight, I should have chosen subjects that complemented my strengths. I'm a creative person, but I pushed that to one side (or made it a hobby) for more 'conventional' subjects, you know, like the Sciences, Maths, etc.

You see...I wanted to be a lawyer. I wanted to fight for the underdog as a profession and had gone to the careers centre when I was eleven (yep...I was THAT kid!) and asked them what I needed to be one. I was a planner even at that tender age! It was totally the wrong direction for me, but I persisted because I'm stubborn and had convinced myself it was what I wanted to do. So, I decided to go to college and retake some of my GCSEs. I passed...so now what?

The universe already had plans for me.

Freshly out of college, life took an unexpected turn. I was seventeen when I fell pregnant. I'd had zero symptoms, and then found out I was pregnant about four and a half months in. My choices were limited. Well, that's what I was told. For me, there was no choice to be made. I was having a baby, and I would figure it all out. My mantra is, 'there's always a way' so I figured it applied to this too. I loved the father of my child, he loved me and we would be in it together. In October 1993 I became a mum, at eighteen-years-old to a beautiful baby boy. The love of my life. I was still living at home at the time, and things started to get a little strained what with me being a new mum and my parents going through a divorce. But, I'm the type of person who gets on with it, no matter the situation or circumstance. This was no different. It was tough.

I had some idea of what I was doing, but when you are a parent, especially a young one, people around you start to tell you you're doing it wrong. 'You're not putting the nappy on right', 'You don't do it like that!', 'Oh... just let me do it'.

I mean...gosh, can you let a girl breathe?

People say it takes a village...umm yeah, sure it does...to drive you bat-crap crazy and running for the hills! Not a single person had an encouraging or positive thing to say to me, and that went on for a while. It was a really tough time, but I took the blows. I sucked it up because my priorities were set in stone — to make sure my child was ok.

That was all that mattered.

Being a young mum has many advantages. You are usually at your peak health so running around after a little one is not as taxing. Generally, life hasn't jaded you yet, and when your child hits adulthood, you are still in your prime. Score!

But there are also significant disadvantages too. People treat you like a child. You get judged and made to feel inferior. Your choices are questioned. The list goes on. So, a big shout out to the fantastic young parents out there. I see you. You are doing great!

When my son was a little over six months old, I became a single parent. Goodbye family unit, hello singledom. I felt completely alone. Heartbroken, discombobulated, and out of sorts. It was just me and the little one against the world.

I moved out of the family home and set myself up in a council house, an empty one! We had a roof over our head but nothing much more. I tried to claim a loan from the government, but that got rejected three times. I wasn't asking for much. Just £400 to kit out an entire two-bedroom house. I thought my request was pretty conservative given that other people around me had obtained housing grants and loans of more than £1000 each without even asking. But they still said no.

It's times like that when you know who your friends are. An old school friend had heard about my situation and offered me her sofa bed. It was a simple gesture, but it meant everything to me. I am eternally grateful! We had something to sit on and a bed to sleep in again, and there was an overwhelming feeling of relief and hope. The optimist in me saw it as a fresh start to our new life. It felt good.

I wasn't giving up. I needed to make our house a home. I was looking for work, but in the meantime, I fought the system. I was going to get that loan! It took weeks of interviews, justification essays, more interviews, a whole load of forms, an escalation to the tribunal and so much hoop-jumping that I briefly considered putting myself into a dog show competition...but I won.

A whopping £250, that I had to pay back!

It almost made up for the fact that I was asked to justify why I needed a fridge when I lived within walking distance (15 minutes) from a supermarket *facepalm* and having my essay questioned because it was too 'articulate' (I kid you not!) ...yeah, it almost made up for it.

And that's how my life as a single parent started. With an empty house, £250, a hand-me-down sofa bed and a determination to make it work. I was always conscious of the fact that I was a 'statistic' – young, black and a single mother. I had the trifecta, but I wasn't going to let that define who I was and how I chose to live my life.

The thing is...I couldn't survive off my moral fortitude, we needed to eat. I was on income support (government funding) and getting milk vouchers and barely surviving. There were times when I could only afford to feed my son, and I went without. Those vouchers were a godsend though, because I could buy other items with it like nappies and baby food. I got everything I could get out of that money but I needed to do better.

Throughout all of this, I continued to study. It was not an option for me to quit. Being able to educate myself, to live a decent life and to provide for my son, were my key motivators. I was the breadwinner. My ex-boyfriend was MIA when it came to providing regular financial support towards the raising of his son, so I found a childminder, worked part-time and studied full-time too. I hated leaving him. I was torn between doing what I knew was the right thing – continuing my education – and feeling guilty because I wasn't at home all day, every day. (Well hello there, rock and a hard place, back again I see). But my son was perfectly happy and oblivious to mummy's conflicted mental state.

Sidenote – I know I'm not alone in this. Especially to the women out there. Who has had to push their feelings aside and either dealt with them later or worse, not at all, because you have a child or children to look after and they take precedence, right? Sucks doesn't it?

I've lost count of the number of times I've wanted to cry or scream into a pillow but had to wait until after my parental duties had subsided, like after they've gone to bed. We rarely get a respite, so dealing with our emotional state gets put on the back burner. 'No time for an emotional breakdown right now...little Timmy needs me to pull the Lego from out of his nose for the fourth time this morning'. I feel you!

I studied and studied. In fact, I studied for the first ten years of my son's life. Looking back, I think I lost my sense of direction and who I was, to an extent. I knew the type of person I was, but I struggled with what I wanted out of life, what kind of job and if I wanted a career, things like that. I realise now that I wasn't actually very career-minded, not in the conventional sense. I always wanted to have a good job and do a good job. I wasn't sure what that would be, but I knew that it would come from a place of service.

I studied Business Admin, Legal Secretarial, Legal (Paralegal) Executive, Psychology and finally ended up with a degree in Criminology and Contemporary Culture. Throughout all of this, I worked two part-time jobs because no one else was going to put food on the table.

No rest for the wicked.

Getting into university was one of the most frustrating and upsetting things I have ever done. I was accustomed to the whole hoop-jumping for the government (woof), so I was prepared for that. But what I didn't expect was to have to fight for my place, to justify why I deserved to go to university and no longer be a burden to the tax-paying society (Seriously?).

I had to obtain documents from the benefits agency to add to my uni application. What should have been a simple transaction of me providing info and them providing me with the relevant document, turned into a dalliance with a woman who relished the power her job gave her, making me feel like complete and utter crap, to the point that she made me cry (with zero remorse given). It took six weeks and with every week's passing, it felt like university might not be on the cards for me. However, thanks to one fateful day when the 'lady who shall not be named' wasn't in the office, her efficient colleague processed my request and I received my document, which allowed me to apply to uni with less than a week to spare from the deadline. Phew!

Doing my degree, working, and being a single parent, was beyond challenging. I forever felt that I was spreading myself thin and that I was never really able to put my all into anything. I was running on empty most of the time, burning the midnight oil. On a good day I survived off about four hours sleep and was in a perpetual haze from being on constant autopilot. Wake up, take son to school, go to uni, go to the library, go to work number one (call centre), pick up son from school, drop him off at his aunt's, go to work number two (cleaning offices), pick son up, go home, spend time with him, put him to bed, pull out my uni work and study. That was basically my life, on a loop for about four years.

Yes I know, the average timeframe for a degree is three years in the UK. Well...mine took four. It was four years because I failed my first year. *gasp!* Yep, totally my fault. I was unable to manage my time. I also wanted to have some fun as a uni student (£1 shots at the student bar...would be rude not to), and so it all got a bit much for me to handle. Plus, I had just gotten Sky television, and they were showing a daily soap opera called Sunset Beach. Think of it as a beachside version of The Bold and the Beautiful. I was hooked!

I regret nothing! But it did set me back a year. It was all good though because I learned a valuable lesson. I repeated my first year, smashed it, and then carried on to graduate with honours with my family and son there to cheer me on. Throughout uni, my need to help people remained and I ended up being a mentor to first-year students. Looking after them throughout the year, answering their questions, lending an ear when needed. You'd think I already had enough things on my plate...I'll never learn!

There I was. Degree, done. Ready to take the next step.

Now what?

It was at that point that I decided to listen to my eight-year-old self and look for a life outside of the UK. You see, when I was eight, I had proclaimed I wouldn't always live in the UK, and that my life was destined for pastures new. Manchester has never felt like home. Fab place to visit but not somewhere I wanted to stay in forever.

Living in the UK was also too damn hard. I was surrounded by people with mindsets that differed to mine. I wasn't content to be born, live, work, and die (with the occasional holiday) in the same place. I felt like I couldn't get ahead and that I was struggling for everything. For me, it always felt like I was taking one step forward and three steps back. I was not getting anywhere. I was miserable, and it was not the best environment to bring up my son. We needed a fresh start and a new life.

In 2005, I packed up everything and moved my son and me to Luxembourg. First, I actually did some research (you know me!) and tried to figure out schooling, where we should live, job vacancies, and stuff like that. Then I left my son with his dad for a couple of months. I had saved enough money to survive for eight weeks. I found an apartment so I had my accommodation sorted, and then I basically had eight weeks to find a job. I found one in six weeks, and the rest is history.

Moving to a country where you don't speak the language has its own challenges. Luxembourg is no different. There are three official languages, French, German and Luxembourgish. I knew some French, but not really enough to get by. I had zero knowledge of German or Luxembourgish, so things got a little complicated on occasion. However, there is a large expat community which made integration easier. Over the years there I brushed up on my French, and attempted to learn German and Luxembourgish. I did ok, until the moment I left and promptly forgot it all. Stoopid brain!

I put my son into a private school. He was eleven and at the start of Secondary age, so possessed no second-language skills. Private schooling was the only place he could go as they had English speaking classes. It wasn't cheap, and my job was barely getting us by. My ex, who promised to pay half, had gone back on his word the moment the wheels hit the tarmac upon arrival (surprise surprise).

As per usual I was on my own.

Luxembourg is all about the conventional family. When the school got a load of me...well let's just say things didn't go so well. They were used to Mummy, Daddy, and a couple of kids, the whole nuclear family shebang. Daddy worked for a bank (that paid for the school fees), and Mummy was either part of the PTA or at the very least at their beck and call and always there to pick up their kids after school in their high end four-by-four (or the nanny if they were so inclined).

And me? They didn't really know what to do with me. They didn't like me. I messed with their cookie cutter 1950s ideals. They disliked I was a working mum, and I couldn't drop everything and be at their beck and call. There were actually two single parents in the whole of the school at the time. Thankfully we found each other and so did our boys, and neither of us paid any attention to those too stuck in their ways to care.

Working in Luxembourg was a whole different ball game. For the most part, it was great. I worked for English speaking companies, or at the very least everyone in my office spoke English. For the first couple of years I was made redundant a fair few times. The last one in, first one out, and all that jazz. It made becoming stable a real challenge because, well, I wasn't. Going from agency to agency, business to business, hoping that this one would stick and I would be there for a while was a little demoralising. But ever the consummate optimist, I always went into each position with gusto and made sure I built some kind of legacy there. Even if it was only for a few months. Finally, in 2010 I started working at a global company. I loved it! I loved the people, I loved the camaraderie, I loved the morale. Things were good...until they weren't. But you already know about that.

Nevertheless, over the years I learnt so much. About business, relationships, life and myself. I wouldn't change it for the world because those are the things that has shaped who I am today and who I will be in the future. For that I thank them.

I lived in Luxembourg for a little over thirteen years, and if anyone ever asks where I'm from I instinctively say Luxembourg, which is strange because I'm from Manchester (can't get rid of that accent!) and I was born there. I'm from England...but my heart is in Luxembourg, it's home and always will be. But now my life has changed yet again, and I'm trying to find my way, my rhythm and my place in this location-independent life.

Should I have a base and then pop back to it once in a while?

Should I just hop from one country to the next until I find one I want to reside in for a few months or longer?

Should I even carry on with this life?

At the moment, I've settled on spending a few months in different places. These first few months of going back and forth from place to place have shown me how exhausting it can all be. Fun but taxing. Constantly being on the move is not good for me and I need to slow it down a little. Spending a month or so in one place is better for me, for now... My main focus at this time is to build my business. Getting out there and helping as many women as I possibly can. Which brings us right back around to my business rebirth and rebrand.

I made a conscious decision to invest in myself and my business this year. I've said yes to pretty much every opportunity that has come my way. I took the time to step back and think about what it takes to succeed in business. Once I figured out what could work for me, I took action to make it happen. Which meant surrounding myself with people who share the same ideals as me. People who can take me to the next level with their expertise and leadership, people who are at the top of their game.

I needed to find my brand voice, so I put myself on a course led by a well-known copywriter. I wanted clarity on how to brand myself and my business, so I got myself a brand architect. I sought additional skills and a business blueprint to upscale, so I got myself a coach. I even went a step further and attended a business retreat where I was in the company of some of the most successful six and seven figure earning female entrepreneurs.

I genuinely believe that if you surround yourself with people that are aligned with you, they will not only elevate you, they will also encourage you to become your best self. This is all a work in progress and should be rinsed and repeated every few months regardless of where you are in your business. You are always evolving, forever changing.

There is never a time to rest on your laurels.

Take my rebrand for example. I'm calling it a rebirth because for me this is the beginning. A whole new outlook, a new approach to my business. I want to build something I'm proud of, and that resonates with the people that I help. I've put my myself into it. Something I think I neglected to do in my earlier incarnations. I'm embracing who I am, and I am putting myself out there. It's a fact that I'm a nerdette, enjoy reading comic books and attending comic cons (comic book conventions), have a blast meeting celebrities and getting their autograph, geeking out on productivity tools, am an obsessive planner, wear my heart on my sleeve and a bunch of other things. It's all me.

As is my love for travel and my digital nomad journey. It's my mission, no... my calling, to empower women to live their best lives, whatever that might be. But I would love to help women who dream of living a nomadic life. Is that you? Want some unsolicited advice?

Know thyself!

I've seen a lot of women out there embark on a nomadic journey and falter at the first hurdle. Why? Because they haven't really thought it through and weren't aligned with their 'why', their reason for doing it in the first place. Taking off because you aren't happy in your life is understandable but let's face it if you aren't happy in one place, how are you going to be happy in another? That's not to say you can't pack a bag, head to Bali, find a beach bar, plant yourself there and drink from a coconut (I highly recommend it, it's delish!) but are you doing so as a form of escapism or do you have a plan to go with that umbrella-topped beverage?

It's worth taking a bit of time to think about what your desire to escape means. This is where having the right mindset is vital. Digital Nomadism is a lifestyle, and it's not for the faint-hearted. Understanding your strengths and weaknesses is so crucial because it could mean the making or breaking of you. I know, I know...it all sounds very dramatic but trust me it's better for you in the long run or all of your efforts could be for naught. Having the right mindset is the foundation upon which you build and reshape yourself and your life. It's worth it!

Take it in baby steps. It can be lonely out there sometimes. So being comfortable sitting alone in a restaurant or a bar helps. I started travelling alone out of necessity. I got fed up of waiting for friends to get themselves together every time we agreed to travel somewhere. Like clockwork, it never happened, and I was left staying at home wishing that I had just gone without them.

Until one day I did just that.

Italy 2006. I went to Rome for a long weekend. I hit the usual tourist spots, ate out (once), drank some excellent wine and sampled the gelato (when in Rome...). I had a nice enough time, but I was fully aware of how alone I was. I had no one to share the experience with. No one to regale on the day's activities. It was a little sad, and I felt a bit isolated. I didn't like it. So, I decided to do something about it. I knew I wanted to travel more and that I was probably going to be doing it alone (for the most part) so I set myself little challenges, like to sit in a bar for an hour and have a drink, to go out for dinner without a distractor (no book, or magazine, not even my phone), and to have a conversation with a stranger. That last one is especially tough for me because contrary to what a lot of people think, I am actually quite shy and introverted. I rarely make the first move to start a conversation.

There have been times where my shyness has brought me so much anxiety and unease that I've cried! But for the most part, I did have quite a savvy strategy in place. I would attach myself to extroverts. They would do most of the heavy lifting, and then I would just slink in like I'd been there the whole time. Works every time! But I still needed to push myself a little and make some kind of effort. I don't always succeed, and I'm still working on it. However, those times where I have felt particularly brave and managed to pluck up the courage to say 'hello' to someone or even strike up a conversation, has paid off and I've gotten to meet some fantastic people.

If you can weather the challenges (and I know you can), you will thrive and have an amazing life, full of magical moments, stories and connections. Know that change can happen if you want it. Anything is possible, even if you start small. There's no reason to go big from the start. Don't get me wrong, dreaming big, thinking big and going big is amazing and empowering, and if you are strong enough to go down that route that's fantastic, you do you, boo! But it's not always realistic and doable and that's okay.

Take one day at a time. Start to think about making a plan. Write things down. Those dreams are not going anywhere if they remain in your head. Writing things down helps you to become clearer on your goals, forms your mindset and gives you something to work towards and look forward to. Start to visualise your future. Once you can see, you can start to move towards it.

I can't emphasise enough just how vital it is to be around people who inspire you. My aunts are my inspiration, each and every one of them (I have seven). I was fortunate enough to be born into a family full of strong (black) women. Women who hold their own, stand their ground, take whatever life throws at them and deal with it like it's everyday work! They do it with unbridled grace, gumption, and beauty and without complaint. They're crazy (I still can't handle partying with them!), forever cracking a joke and smiling and they are freaking awesome! I heart them so much!

They were the first strong women I'd ever encountered. Growing up, I never really idolised anyone, but I did have admiration for my aunts and two other ladies too... Wonder Woman and Princess Leia. I was into Disney also, like many little girls, but I don't ever recall wanting to be a Princess like Sleeping Beauty or Cinderella. I wanted to fight for justice like Diana and Leia. Even back then I understood the strength and compassion they exuded. The way Wonder Woman cared so deeply for others resonated with me, so it's no wonder (no pun intended) that I named my business after her or why I've started the She Power Movement. But I never actually really wanted to be her, or Leia. I wanted to be me, infused with elements of the women I admired. I still do.

Being around people that make you want to be the best version of yourself, is what we all should strive for, because it inspires you to be that person for someone else, and they someone else. And so the wheel of empowerment goes on and on.

Which is why I'm really excited about the direction my business is going, in terms of supporting female entrepreneurs and being with them on their journey of growth and success. Working together to become our authentic selves is how we change the world for the better.

Who's with me?

ABOUT THE AUTHOR

Cassandra is many things: a woman, a mother, a comic geek, a digital nomad. The list could go on for miles without covering each facet of her ever-changing world. She created her business, Wonder Assist, on International Women's Day, with the intent of helping to guide and support action-taking, driven female entrepreneurs through their professional and personal journeys.

Having been inspired by Wonder Woman, her favourite comic character, and all things She Power, crafting the idea of supporting amazing female entrepreneurs by using her offline support skills in the online world was a natural step.

The road she's travelled hasn't always been easy. It's required her to develop She Powers of her own: the ability to traverse through adversity as a young, single mother, embrace change when being made redundant in a role she thrived in, and a positive outlook despite a new-found chronic illness diagnosis.

As an Entrepreneurial Support Specialist, Cassandra leverages her wealth of experience as a Personal Assistant in the corporate world and her life experiences gained through travel. Her mission is to unleash the She Power of every female entrepreneur that is putting in crazy hours, struggling to manage their workload and/or family and wishing that they had a more productive and profitable business by supporting, organising, simplifying and reducing their workload, their mind and their life.

CASSANDRA QUEELEY

Virtual Assistant Wandress for Creative Female Entrepreneurs.
www.wonderassist.com

- @wonderassist (business)
- @shepowermovement (group)
- @wonderassist
- @cassandraqueeley
- Group: **www.linkedin.com/groups/8710811**

Joyce Hardie

CHAPTER 9
Old, Sick and AMAZING!
By Joyce Hardie

"Grant me the serenity to accept things I cannot change, courage to change the things I can and the wisdom to know the difference."

My earliest memory is of me lying in bed with my dad. There were lots of strangers walking back and forwards around the house. Everyone seemed really busy, but I had no idea what was going on. I was five-years-old, and all I wanted was my mum. Dad told me that everyone was there to help Mum and soon I was going to have a new brother or sister to play with, something I had always looked forward to. I can remember the wave of excitement and the buzz all around as we waited to hear if it was a boy or a girl.

We grew up in a pretty normal household. Mum and Dad both worked but there was always one of them at home to look after us, at least until we were old enough to look after ourselves, or at least until I was old enough to look after my baby sister. By that time though, as much as I adored her, I didn't want to play with her anymore.

In primary school, I was one of the smart kids. I got involved in everything that was going on, from playing netball to singing 'Raindrops Keep Falling on my Head', at a school concert. I can even remember the original version was written by Hal David & Burt Bacharach for the movie Butch Cassidy and the Sundance Kid.

I can remember going on a school cruise during my primary years. There were two cruise ships, Uganda and Nassau. If you're from my generation, you'll probably know all about them, because either you went on one of the cruises or know someone who did.

I remember visiting Pompeii, Athens, Crete, Carthage, and Malta! Sounds gorgeous, doesn't it!

But it was horrific, absolutely horrific.

I was incredibly seasick, as were two-thirds of the other kids on the ship. The sea was really rough. We were supposed to dock in Alexandria to visit Cairo, but it was too stormy for the boats to bring us into the harbour. That year was the worst weather in the Mediterranean for twenty-five years, and as a result, we were stuck offshore in the middle of this horrendous storm until someone made the decision to divert the ship to Malta.

Being on the ship during a storm was awful. You had to go below deck to sleep and to get food from the canteen. Your food tray had indents for the different courses, and you staggered along the galley with it, trying to keep your feet stable on the rolling ship. The crew fired the food at you, and it all ended up as one sloppy mess. The smell was absolutely gross, and my stomach rebelled. Even thinking about it now makes my stomach heave.

All the cabins were below deck. It was ridiculously cramped, smelly, and dark. It was horrible. I sneaked up onto the deck to get some air. We weren't supposed to go up there because it was so stormy, but I just needed air so desperately. I found this little alcove where I found a bit of shelter from the wind and battering rain. I huddled up as best as I could and tried to stop myself from vomiting.

I don't know how long I sat there, but it must have been for hours. Eventually, the door I had been leaning against, opened and a man I didn't know was standing there. He was incredibly kind, especially when I expected to get into trouble for being on deck. He asked me how I was feeling, and when I told him I thought I was going to die, he replied, 'That's what seasickness does to you.'

You start off feeling like you're going to die and when you can't get off the ship and escape from it, you hope you will die.

I never got over the feeling that seasickness causes, and ever since I've avoided going on boats, that is, until 2010 when eruptions of Eyjafjallajökull, a volcano in Iceland, erupted, causing enormous disruption to air travel across western and northern Europe for about six days. We were in Portugal at the time and came home overland with a thirty-six-hour bus trip through Spain and France, and then an eight-hour ferry trip from France to Plymouth. This was done under total duress and with a few bottles of red wine to stop me thinking about it! Most importantly I did survive the crossing, but I still won't be rushing to do it again anytime soon.

Instead of going to Egypt as planned, they took us to Malta . Once we had docked and were on dry land again, it was amazing; I remember how great it felt because we hadn't planned to stop, there hadn't been any organised excursions. We were told to 'go off in wee groups...you've gotta be back here for,' and I'll never forget it, 'four o'clock.' And so four of us went off to explore Valletta together, which was great after being cooped up on the ship. After a while, we looked at our watches and decided it was time to get back on the boat. Once we reached the port, we started running because we knew we might be a little bit late. The ship was just around the next corner so we knew we'd make it, just!

However, we turned the corner...no ship. We went round the next corner... no ship. Now you can't hide a ship. They're enormous. We kept running and turning corner after corner. No ship! We then started to panic, thinking they were gonna leave us behind. And then rationality kicked in, and we reassured each other they wouldn't. But four o'clock came and went, and we started to get hysterical. We had stitches in our sides from running. Everyone was in a state of absolute panic.

Eventually, we turned this corner, and there was the ship, with everybody standing at the bottom shouting at us because we were holding everything back. We were in floods of tears, from the fear and relief, but still, we got into trouble. We felt such a relief that we were safe and that the ship hadn't gone without us. Then I just felt angry, after all, we were just kids and they had let us go off in a strange country by ourselves. They were blaming us for not getting back on time, going on and on about how much it would cost the shipping company.

No one seemed to realise we were really scared and had believed they would actually leave without us. I think that was when I realised I needed to ensure I always had money tucked away in my purse, that I could use for a taxi to get me home. I still do that today. Back in those days, no one asked how you felt, or if you wanted to talk about what happened. It was, 'Get on with it. You should have been here. No excuses.' So, we did get on with it.

It's funny because my memories of that cruise have led to two things. My travel bug, which has taken me to many countries and many different adventures. But I've never been a fan of package deals and tours, because you need to be in certain places at certain times...Maybe I was traumatised because of that ship. I don't know. I'd rather do my own thing in my own timescales! And the second thing was that I definitely hate boats!

At secondary school I wasn't one of the smartest kids in my year, I was more average, but I was never stupid. At that point, I probably became even more introverted than I had been. I was quite a plain kid with buck teeth and glasses, and I was incredibly nervous, which got me into trouble because I laughed when I was nervous and teachers didn't like that.

I had some great times with my group of friends, like listening to David Bowie's Changes and burning incense sticks, and then sneaking out to the payphone on the corner to phone the boys we liked. I remember sitting my O levels (Standard Grades today). When our results arrived, I was in Torquay, as my friend's mum had taken me on holiday with them. As both of us had passed with flying colours, Fiona's mum paid for us to go to see a fortune teller as a treat. I didn't really believe in fortune tellers, but I was curious, maybe some people could tell the future. It was like when you first found out that Santa Claus isn't real, but you want to keep believing in case he is real and doesn't bring you presents because you don't believe in him! We both agreed we wouldn't say anything that would give her any information about us, just to test her.

This was really exciting because we were still quite young so what could she tell us? There are certain things she said to me that stuck in my mind. She told me that I'd received big news in a letter, but I hadn't opened it. Someone else had opened the letter and told me what was in it by phone. This was true because I'd phoned my mum to get her to open my results so I wouldn't have to wait until I got home. We didn't have a text or email service in those days.

The fortune teller described a boy to me, a boy I was really into, and told me that he wasn't interested in me (I knew that bit!). She said, 'He'll come back and he'll want to try and make a go of it with you. And you'll tell him to get lost because you'll be with someone else.' I thought no way. If he came back, I would be all over him like a rash. That certainly wasn't going to happen. But it did. We had been out at the pub with a whole load of different people. He walked me home and told me he had been an idiot, and that he really wanted to go out with me. I said no because I was going out with someone else at the time, who is now actually my husband!

The third thing the fortune teller told me was that I would marry a guy that wore a white coat, and that he wasn't a doctor and didn't work in a hospital. That's true because my husband's a chemist. He worked in laboratories, so he wore white lab coats. I must have been fourteen or fifteen at that time and didn't even know someone like that.

After that, the rest of secondary school was pretty okay, with nothing out of the ordinary happening except for one major thing which then impacted the rest of my life.

I left school at the end of the fifth year, but on the 5th of March 1977, three months before the end of my school career, I went out on my first date with Alex, who is now my husband. Forty-one years ago. For a few months before that my friends and his friends hung around in the same places, but Alex and I had never spent time on our own. In March, he asked me out on a date. We went to see a Pink Panther film at a cinema that's now long gone, then we went for something to eat at a local Chinese restaurant, which isn't there anymore either. I found out, a long time after that, that Alex had taken me out for a bet. His pals bet him a half bottle of vodka that he wouldn't go out with me. He did it just to get a half bottle of vodka. Not a romantic start but there must've been something good about it because we're still together forty-one years later.

Alex was the year above me at school and did a sixth year. At the end of the school year, Alex went to Glasgow University, and I headed to Paisley College of Technology, which is now the University of West of Scotland. I wanted to do a social work qualification, and Paisley was one of the few places that did that qualification. I knew from quite early on that I wanted to help people, and social work seemed like a logical way of doing that.

Student life was great doing all the things that students do, such as, drinking, partying, more drinking and a little bit of studying. I loved some of my course, especially psychology and social geography, but I hated economics and politics. I don't have a logical brain, so these things just didn't appeal. It was the softer, touchy-feely things I enjoyed.

During this time, I moved away from my mum and dad's house into a rented flat. My mum was distraught, but my dad and I just didn't get on, so it seemed the best thing to do. My flatmate was a friend from school, so we got on ok and enjoyed our independence. Oh, apart from when the cooker caught fire, three weeks into the tenancy and the landlord took weeks to get it replaced. I was petrified my mum would find out because I was sure she'd make me move back home. So instead of telling her, we just lived off sandwiches and cold snacks!

In July 1980, at the age of twenty, I graduated with a BA in Applied Social Studies. I remember that day distinctly. I was wearing a black velvet skirt suit with my robes and a green and gold hood. I graduated in Paisley Abbey, watched by my mum and dad and Alex. Then we came back to Glasgow to visit my gran just to show her my robes. We also took lots of photographs to make her feel part of the day.

At the grand old age of twenty, I found out that you had to be twenty-one before you could start the social qualification. I was devastated, but everyone kept telling me that I was young and that taking a year out would be good for me, and that I could go back to studying the following year. I didn't have any choice, so all I had to do was to find something to pass my time for a year. I tried care homes and children's homes to get myself some experience, but I couldn't work there either because I wasn't yet qualified!

I just wanted something that would pay my rent! While I had been studying, I had worked part-time in a huge department store in Glasgow, called Goldbergs. I had started working there at Christmas, a few years before that as a Christmas elf, and then once Christmas was over, I had carried on working in the children's department at the weekends.

To help resolve my cash flow problem, I asked them if I could work some extra hours. Something that would give me some money during this time off. They said yes and gave me a full-time job working in the accounts payable department. I was basically taking all of the transactions with their suppliers and just reconciling that against the supplier's invoice before paying them.

I absolutely hated it, numbers, numbers and more numbers...my worst nightmare. Because my heart wasn't in it, I was always getting into trouble for wasting time and not doing things properly...did I check this, were those figures correct? I wasn't interested, and eventually, they realised it wasn't my thing and transferred me to another department.

The business, at that time, had just launched its own credit card and they wanted me to be involved in setting it up, and I absolutely loved it! It was amazing. The only numbers involved were customer numbers as the credit card started to take off. When I started, there was a tiny little box of cardholders; over my time with the business, it grew into hundreds of thousands. By the time I left the company, something like a quarter of a million people had these cards.

I loved that job and never did go back to study for a social work qualification. In the end, I stayed there for ten years. During that time, Alex and I travelled all over the world. We were both earning and had no real liabilities apart from my rent. Life was amazing and then Alex got sick, really sick.

We went on holiday to Morocco and stayed in mud-hut style accommodation. It sounded authentic and, it actually was a mud-hut. It was tiny inside with walls that were three feet high. It had a pyramid-shape thatched roof, and there was a piece of string across the whole hut for you to hang your clothes over. And for beds, there were two wafer-thin mattresses to lie on. I mean, they were biscuit thin and very, very uncomfortable. Because there was a shortage of water, they only turned it on at night so if you wanted a shower, you had to get up at four o'clock in the morning because they turned the water off at 4.30 am.

We stayed in there for two weeks. There wasn't much to do but laze about and go to the bar and appreciate the local hospitality. On our last night, we went out for a meal with another couple we had met, and as you weren't allowed to bring the money out of the country, we had to spend all that we had. And so, the four of us had a great night out, with lots of food and drinks.

The next day we were sitting on the plane flying to Manchester when Alex said, 'I don't feel well' and my reaction was, 'that's your own fault then, isn't it? You shouldn't have drunk so much when you knew you were traveling home today.'

By the time we got off the plane in Manchester, he felt a bit better, so we went into central Manchester to have breakfast and catch our train home to Glasgow. And that's when things got really bad. Alex wasn't well at all. I spent all my time on the train carrying him back and forward to the toilet. He was barely conscious, and I could see everyone tut-tutting. 'Look at him. He's drunk. That's a disgrace at this time of day.' You could see it all over their faces.

Eventually, a woman passed us and asked me if everything was all right. I told her that I thought something was seriously wrong with him. The woman obviously believed me and went to get the guard, who then came to see him for himself. He agreed that Alex looked really ill but told me that this was a direct inter-city train without a lot of stops. I asked him if he could get a message to Glasgow? I desperately needed to get a message home so that somebody could come and meet us.

The guard went away and then came back and told me to write down the phone number of the person I wanted to get the message to…which was my mum. He said that the train wasn't scheduled to stop at any of the stations, but he said the driver would slow down enough for me to pass a message to someone on the platform. This massive inter-city train pulled into this tiny little station and I gave the man standing on the platform a scrap of paper, which had my mum's work phone number on it, just saying, 'Alex ill. Can someone meet us at the station?'

And the train kept going. Alex was totally out of it at this point and I was thinking all the way home, I've given them the wrong number. That's not my mum's number! But it was the right number and when we got into Glasgow, my mum and dad were there waiting. She had phoned my dad to get the car, and then they called Alex's mum at her work to come as well. The three of them were on the station platform waiting for us. My dad carried Alex off the train, put him in the car, and we went to the Victoria Infirmary hospital. Immediately they rushed him off to examine him, but because he was unconscious, they came to ask me questions so they could work out what was wrong. When they'd heard where we'd been, they transferred him to an ambulance and sent him to the infectious disease unit at Ruchill Hospital in Glasgow.

No one was allowed near him without masks, except me, the logic being that I had been within him so I would have been exposed to the same things as he was. It was crazy. If he read a newspaper, they burned it so no one else could be contaminated. They thought it might have been some sort of strain of malaria. But they couldn't quite put their finger on it. They tested him for absolutely everything under the sun. It was a scary time for all of us. I was actually scared that maybe I had it too. What if it was lying dormant in me ready to come to the surface at any time? I was also afraid that Alex wouldn't get better but I was proud of myself for staying calm and managing to get him the help he needed. That was the time when I realised that I'm great in a crisis and can cope well when things go wrong.

The day I returned to work, I was violently sick, and everyone panicked. Somebody told the head of personnel, who phoned me to say, 'Take as much time off as you need but don't come back until you know what's wrong with him.' I was off for a couple of weeks, which was great because I was fit and healthy and could spend the time at the hospital with Alex. I knew there wasn't anything wrong with me, it was just my body reacting to the stress I had been through bringing Alex home.

I carried on working with Style card, but Alex lost so much time being in and out of hospital that he had to give up doing his PhD and went to work instead. He was frequently in and out of the hospital as they continued to test for different illness and disease, but they never did find out what it was.

By the time Alex and I had been together for around nine years, I raised the conversation about where our relationship was going. Alex thought it was ok as it was and made it plain that he didn't want to get married. But I did. I wanted to get married and have kids. I didn't want to spend my life alone, so we split up. I even suggested that we just live together, which wasn't the norm back in the eighties, but Alex said no because it would cause a rift between my family and me. I was absolutely devastated, and physically in pain. I cried buckets and frequently thought about going back to him, after all, things were great. It wasn't that we didn't get on, it was just that we wanted different things. And I knew that if we carried on, the subject would come up again and again and we would only fight about it.

One day, about ten months after we'd split up, I came home to find a note from Alex's friend's girlfriend saying that Alex was back in hospital and that he wanted to see me. I was so tempted, but what was the point. If we both still wanted different things, it would only stir up all that pain again. By the time I relented and agreed to see him, he was home from the hospital but still bedridden. I felt really nervous going to see him, not sure if I was doing the right thing or not. But I went, and we had the usual chit-chat. How are you feeling? What did the doctors say? What have you been doing? And then totally out of the blue, he asked me to marry him...exactly what I wanted, so I said NO! I told him he was only saying it because he was ill, and that if he still wanted to marry me when he was feeling better, then he should ask again.

Needless to say, I kept going to see him, and once he was better, he asked me to marry him again, and I said YES!

We got married in '86. And as Alex and I are both Christians, we got married in a church, the same one that I had been christened in. On the way to the church in the car, my dad asked if I really wanted to go through with it, and I said of course I did. Then the driver started telling us stories about famous people that he'd had in his car, and that the actual seat I was sitting on, was the same one used by Sean Connery the week before. After the ceremony, we went to a nearby park to get the photographs taken and then onto a local hotel for our reception. By that time, we were starting to relax and were looking forward to an amazing party, and it was. The church service had been about us being married as per God's word, but the reception was about celebrating our marriage with all our friends and family.

It was just a great time, and we had an absolute ball, but halfway through the night, the manager came up to us and said, 'Look, you need to watch. A lot of people are convinced that you're staying in the hotel (which we were!). They are trying to find out what room you are in so that they can play tricks on you. So, just watch what you're doing and make a point of telling everyone that you are leaving.' Alex's friends were incredible pranksters and were hoping to have a laugh at our expense. They had planned to put things into our bed, put joke soap into our bathroom and similar juvenile pranks.

So, that's what we did, we told everyone we were going home but later on that night, Alex said the manager told him we needed to leave and come back later. We weren't pleased about it but thought that if people saw us go, then they would accept that. As we were trying to get a taxi, a work colleague of Alex's offered to give us a lift and dropped us back at the house where we sat on the stairs. The company we bought our sofa and chairs from had gone bust, just before they were due to deliver our furniture, so not only did we not have anything to sit on, we had lost thousands of pounds.

After the excitement of the wedding and the reception, it was an anti-climax to sit on the stairs. With nothing to do, it seemed like we sat there for ages, but in reality, it was about an hour. We then had to go back to the hotel to collect our cases and the car because we were driving to Prestwick Airport the next morning to fly to the United States.

When we finally got in the car to drive to Prestwick, we discovered that somebody had put cooking dye into the windscreen washer water. So, when Alex used the wipers, it spurted out blue. It was such a vivid blue, which was terrifying because we couldn't see out of the windscreen very well. We didn't really have the time to stop and do something about it either, or we would have missed our flight.

But we made it and flew to Shannon in Ireland. As we went through American Immigration, there was a really dour immigration officer who asked why we wanted to go to the States. He seemed totally dismayed when we said it was a honeymoon, like he couldn't fathom why anyone would want to go to America on holiday. He kept asking, 'Why do you want to go to America?' Eventually, he let us through, and we got on with our journey to Florida. To spend any time in America in the 1980s was unusual, but to spend three weeks was absolutely incredible. We stayed at Reddington Beach on the Gulf of Mexico, and it was absolutely fantastic.

Alex loves fishing so he went on a fishing trip one day. I'm pretty much a pool and a book kind of girl, so that day I had a great time relaxing. When Alex came back, he was like the typical hunter bringing his catch home to provide for his new wife, however, in my eyes, he was carrying this horrible, disgusting, manky fish. I wasn't sure what he expected me to do with it, and I said so. Eventually we agreed that he'd take it to the chef to see if he wanted it, and he did. He added it to a barbecue that he was doing that night. We had an amazing time socialising with aircrew who were staying at the hotel. Neither of us ate Alex's fish because neither of us liked fish at that point.

We had a great honeymoon, exploring the whole coast from Clearwater to St. Petersburg and went to Disney for the first time.

My favourite moment was when I received a call from reception asking to speak to Mrs. Hardie. I remember thinking that Alex's mum wasn't there, until I realised they were asking for me! That trip started our love affair with Florida, and we have been back many times, both with and without our daughter and other family members.

Unfortunately, the honeymoon was soon over, and we had to come home and go back to work. I was still working in Style Financial Services, but by this time I was leading the debt management team.

Alex had also started working for a company in Govan, which he ended up owning just under half of. In those days he used to tell me that he didn't understand how I could work for a corporate because of all of the politics, and it was just too much hassle. He liked the way it was, just him and his partner's business plans on the back of a cigarette packet. No hassle, no deals, nothing. I, on the other hand, was part of a corporate which was always full of politics. As time went on, my role continued to change within the company. I project-managed a new financial product, branded cards for different organisations and finally became the Facilities Manager managing all the background services, except IT, which are required for the core business to operate.

Throughout this time Alex and I continued to travel all over the world. We travelled about three times a year because we adored visiting new places, learning about their culture and exploring. Places we visited included Hong Kong, Bangkok, Bali, Hawaii, Greece, Cyprus, Spain. Russia, Bulgaria, to name just a few. And had lots of amazing adventures.

In the summer of 1990, I was approached by a colleague I knew through my work in Goldbergs. He told me he had a client who was looking for an office manager to project manage the construction of a new office and then to manage it. For many reasons, it was the right time to change jobs, after all, my one year stop gap position had lasted 10 years.

Gerry told me it would be an informal chat, rather than an interview with the person he knew in the business, who happened to be the Managing Director. I hadn't been thinking about changing jobs, so I wasn't fussed about whether I got the job or not. I went along to see him feeling pretty relaxed, which probably made me come across more naturally. He was obviously impressed because I was invited me to another interview.

This time, I was also to meet the person who was going to be my boss. She was a lawyer, and from her attitude, I got the feeling she didn't like me. I later found out she was the same with everyone. While I was chatting to this woman, she asked what I did at the moment, so I explained all the different things I did on a day-to-day basis, including managing the mailroom for the style card. I will always remember the way she looked at me and said, 'How difficult can that be, putting stamps on letters?' I was furious and remember thinking, you just don't have a clue. I mean this wasn't just a mail room, it was a team of amazing people who managed to post more than 250K credit card statements in a ten-day period every single month, with other promotions sent out in between. I basically told her that. Then I thought, 'Well that's it. I've blown that, I'm never going to get the job now.'

But they made me a job offer, with a salary and package I could not refuse. They wanted me to project manage the construction of their new headquarters in the centre of Glasgow with a budget of £25.5million. And I said yes! It was incredible. I worked with experts in the construction industry for two years, acting as the main link between them and the business. That's the biggest achievement of my career.

They offered me the job in September 1990 with an October start date. As I was between jobs, we went on holiday again. This time to Canada for a friend's wedding. This was a Scottish guy that Alex had been at university with, who was marrying a Croatian girl who was living in Canada and whose family owned an Italian bakery. Very cosmopolitan. We flew to Toronto, for a wedding filled with customs from both Scotland and Croatia. It was just one night after another. The first night we arrived, Lily's mum and dad had invited us back to their house for dinner. We were shattered and wanted to go back to bed, but we didn't want to upset anyone so we went to have the meal with them.

The following night, Donald's mum put on a meal for everybody who travelled from Scotland. The next night was the stag do and hen night. Both Alex and I went to separate nights out, promising to meet back at the hotel. That was the night I saw the largest pizza I had ever seen in my entire life. First of all, us girls went to Toronto. We went to a couple of different clubs before deciding to go back to our hotel. As we piled out of the cars in the hotel car park, we met the guys who had had the same idea. The girls all went to our room because we had a nice living room as well as a bedroom, and the guys all went to somebody else's room in the hotel. There were a number of phone calls between the rooms and different people.

After the last of the girls had left, there was a knock on our door. I opened the door, expecting to see Alex and there was a guy with a three-foot square pizza. The boys, well Alex, had ordered the largest pizza they could possibly get with absolutely everything on it. It was massive, and cost an arm and a leg which I had to pay. I sat there looking at this huge pizza thinking, 'What am I going to do with this?' I took it down to the room the boys were in and gave it to them and for the rest of the holiday, another four, five days after that, the remnants of the pizza kept appearing outside people's doors in the morning. It became a competition to see who would be left with it at the end of the holiday.

The wedding itself was amazing although some of Lily's Croatian relations were a little bemused by the kilts the boys were wearing at the wedding party, and our two-finger approach to pouring drinks. After the wedding, Alex and I hired a car, and we drove up to Ottawa with one of the other Scottish guests who was there on his own. As it was the autumn in Canada and everything was so beautiful, except we ended up on the police wanted list. The original plan had been to go for a couple of days, but because everything was so beautiful, we phoned to extend the car hire and kept on exploring. It was so good to relax after the hectic week of the wedding. Soon after we were told that the car hire people had reported the vehicle as stolen, and the police were out looking for us. Whoever had taken the call to extend the car hire obviously hadn't updated the records. So after that excitement, we returned to the UK and my new job.

When I had gone for my (not) interview, they had a site in mind that they wanted to develop. By the time I joined them, they had actually bought a different site which was just a big hole in the ground. We started from that hole in the ground, designing the building as quickly as possible so that the construction company didn't stop work or cause the company any financial penalties.

That was when I got my bug for property. I was young, and used to dressing in power suits and stilettos. But all that changed, having to spend time on a building site. The team bought me my own wellington boots and hard hat.

Instead of feeling like a fish out of water in what was a totally male-orientated industry, it worked in my favour. As I walked around the site, the workers, joiners, electricians, and mechanical engineers, all took time to explain to me, not in a condescending way, exactly what they were doing, why they were doing it, and how it would look and work when it was finished. I knew every inch of that building, all 70,474 sq. feet of office space, the plant rooms and car parks. This was my biggest achievement, and I was honoured to take Princess Anne on a tour of the building when she came to perform the official opening.

I had been told that I would manage the building on a day-to-day basis once the project was complete, but by the time the project had finished, they had bought another company and made me interview for my own job against their Facilities Manager. HE got the job! I was bitterly disappointed because it was my building and I wanted to run it. I was, however, put in charge of refurbishing all of our sales branches which were scattered throughout the UK. Several years after the Facilities Manager retired, I was finally given the job and had the horrible task of closing down all of the branches, and by that time I was heavily pregnant.

Alex and I hadn't talked much about having kids, but the assumption was that we would have them one day. However, my body clock was marching on, and we had the, it's now or never, conversation. So, we decided that it would be now.

During that time, I went out regularly with a friend, and we'd have great night out, with lots of food and drink. After one particular night, I was feeling a bit hungover which wasn't unusual. However, this time it went on for four days, I just felt awful, and during those days my sister made an off the cuff remark saying, 'Maybe you're pregnant.' And I was! We were so excited, but I was one of those people who looked pregnant right away and was constantly getting told the old adage, 'You're eating for two now.' So, I did, and put on four stone!

We had agreed that I would go back to work after Kirstie was born, so one afternoon, a week after she was due, we went to visit the nursery which was just around the corner from our house. I felt awful, my back was sore, and I was really uncomfortable. When Alex went back to finish his working day, I tried to rest. But I knew something was going on, so I phoned the hospital who told me that I was in the early stages of labour. They told me to take a bath and to go to hospital when I was having regular contractions five minutes apart. When Alex, came home I was still in the bath. I was too big to try and get out of it by myself! I told him what the hospital had said and got him to time my contractions. I just remember his face going white and him saying, 'Get out the bath, we need to go now!'

My contractions were four minutes apart. When we reached the hospital, I was examined, and they agreed that labour was well-advanced and that I should stay in the hospital. They told Alex they would put me on a Tens machine to manage the pain and help me sleep, and that he should go home and they'd call him if anything happened. That was Monday 3 February 1997. My daughter was born at 4.25 pm on the 6th of February. Kirstie was lying at an angle while in my womb and would never have been able to turn to enable me to have a natural birth, but my consultant said we should wait because she might turn, but she didn't!

On the Wednesday, when my consultant accidentally broke my waters during an examination (I was convinced that my mum was going to murder someone for leaving me so long), they decided to move me to the labour ward. They tell you that when you give birth there will only be your midwife and maybe your consultant. I had half the hospital all deliberating the best way to manage the birth. They were taking blood samples from both myself and the baby, and it was only when they said that the baby, and I, were starting to get distressed, that they decided they would do an emergency C-section. I should mention that through all of this Alex was sitting as far away as possible going greener and greener, he hates the sight of blood. And so our amazing daughter was born. A clone of her father.

I went back to work when Kirstie was six-months-old, as that was all the maternity leave we got. I went through terrible feelings of guilt for leaving her in the nursery, although looking back, Kirstie wasn't too bothered.

For the next few years, everything carried on pretty much as before. The one thing that changed was our holidays. We still went abroad as much as possible, but instead of exciting new places, it was family hotels with kids' clubs. Not that Kirstie ever went to the clubs, she always just wanted to be with us. The exception was at Atlantis in the Bahamas, where Kirstie decided she loved the kids club...at $100 a session we weren't as keen. Kirstie went to the kids' club, and Alex and I went to Subway to save money!

It was early in 2011 that I started to have problems. When I woke up in the morning, my fingers would be really achy and sore, but I initially put it down to age, arthritis or rheumatism or something like that. But over the next few months, it got worse. I was having problems with my feet, and my neck and shoulders. I had aches and pains everywhere. Eventually, in the summer of that year, I went to see my GP who was a bit concerned. She suggested that if I had private medical insurance, I should use it to see a consultant, as it would be quicker than waiting for the NHS. Luckily, I had medical insurance as part of my package in work. I made an appointment with a neurologist, and then a rheumatologist, who recommended another specialist, and then another specialist. I was so scared. This went on for months, but no one that I saw could find anything wrong with me. They kept taking more and more bloods, more tests.

Before they had worked out what was going on in my body, we received an enormous medical bill. Thinking it was a mistake, I phoned the insurers who advised that unless you have a diagnosis, the insurance cover was capped at £1000. Because I hadn't had a diagnosis, they wouldn't pay the bills. In the end, we had to pay thousands of pounds for all the tests that had been done. It was back to my GP to get put back into the NHS system. In the meantime, I was prescribed lots of medication and left to get on with it. I was so tired, it was like living in a fog, forgetting things. I was so scared and very sore, and I just needed someone to tell me what was happening to me.

While we were awaiting a confirmed diagnosis, normal life went on in the background. Over the years, my job didn't really change much. I worked in that building. I ran that building. The only changes came every time we were bought out, or our parent company changed their name. Finally, we were bought by The Pearl Group, who had their head offices in London. They wanted London premises for the Investment Management arm of the business too. I spent two to three days every week searching for new premises in London, managing the refurbishment and relocations and eventually the day-to-day running of the premises. The budget was just silly money, and we managed to create an absolutely, really high end, quality office environment, overlooking St. Paul's Cathedral. Another job to be proud of.

Those times were quite hard; I absolutely adored what I was doing in London. It was my passion, but I hated being away from Alex and Kirstie. Especially, when Kirstie was young. As she became a teenager, I became her arch enemy, and she took all of her temper tantrums out on me.

I blamed it on myself, thinking if I could be there more maybe we could sort out our differences.

There were lots of slamming doors, leaving me tired and frequently in tears. I tried to work out what I could do to change things, but my schedule was gruelling. I was up at 4am on a Monday morning to catch the first flight to London, and in the office before 9am. I would work until about 7pm.

On Tuesday mornings I was back in the office by 7am and if I was lucky, I'd get a flight back to Glasgow about 5pm and get home between 7 and 8 pm. I then worked full time in Glasgow for three days, catching up on things that I should have done while I was in London. I did that for three years. During this time, my health got worse, and my medication increased time and time again. It was a tough time, and I struggled so much with everything. My health was terrible, and I felt like a rubbish mum. I didn't know what to do about any of it.

During this period, Alex was facing his own struggles. They had sold the company because his partner wanted to retire, and with a young child, Alex didn't want us take on the loans that would have been required to buy his partner out. But a bit like in my own situation, the business was sold on again and Alex got to the stage where he hated work. He just absolutely hated getting up in the morning, and to go there. Then, one day out of the blue, a contact that he knew offered him a job in Dubai.

It was a fantastic opportunity and sounded exciting, but when we talked about it, we knew he would have to go on his own. Our daughter was still at school and had two years of important exams before she went off to University. So, we agreed that Kirstie and I would stay in the UK for two years and then we would revisit the situation. I thought that once Kirstie went to University, I'd move to Dubai to be with Alex and start a new chapter in our lives in the sunshine.

In May 2012, Alex moved to Dubai, and a month later I was, finally, diagnosed with Fibromyalgia and chronic fatigue. It was a real horrendous time. My condition was managed with more medication, but I was still in pain most days, and still working full-time.

Kirstie was studying hard, and missing the support of her dad, despite regular Skype calls. I struggled to come to terms with Alex being away too, and the fact that I had a very painful illness for which there is no cure. I had no idea how I could change this. I wanted to be fit and healthy and provide support to Kirstie, but I also needed my husband to be there to help and support me and the crazy illness which was slowly becoming my primary focus each day.

Thanks to a friend, I reconnected with my faith.

My faith had taken a back seat after Kirstie was born. Working full-time, and part of every week in London, the weekends were the only time I had to do housework, so church-going became pretty irregular for me. My friend slowly helped me to reconnect with God, and to use my faith to deal with my health problems and our disjointed family life. We have shared a lot of tears and laughter over the years, and I don't know how I would have got through the early days without her. I will be eternally grateful for her friendship in what was a horrible time in my life.

In the summer of 2013, I got a nasty viral infection, which totally floored me. For the first few days, I couldn't move. And then, when I was well enough to get out of bed, I was still in significant pain and unable to do much.

Before the virus, I had been working on a refurbishment project, and after a few weeks, we agreed I would continue to work on it from home. The architects were happy to send documents and drawings and everything to me, and we chatted via conference calls. I was happy. I had a diversion from daytime television and I could work when I felt well enough. It was mostly phone calls, so it wasn't anything strenuous.

One day, the architect phoned mid-morning to ask if I was all right. I assured him that I was just the same and that nothing had changed. He then told me that he had been called in for a meeting with the Project Sponsor, who had told him, that under no circumstances was he to contact me because my doctor had said that I wasn't to do any work whatsoever. I was really confused because this was totally untrue.

Later that day, my boss phoned to say that HR had been on the phone, and they weren't happy with me working because I wasn't covered by insurance when I was off ill. That actually made sense, but I couldn't understand why external parties had been given an entirely different story. But literally from that date on, apart from the HR manager who came out to see me, not one single person in that company got in touch with me. I had worked there for twenty-three years at this point. There were no Christmas cards, no phone calls, nothing. I later heard that everyone had been told under no circumstances were they to contact me at the request of my doctor.

At the end of February on 2014, I officially left the company. I subsequently found out that there had been a staff collection, and a card was passed round for everyone to sign, but someone stole not only the money but the card too. I was hurt and angry about the way I was treated, but at the end of the day, they did me a massive favour.

The following month, I did a couple of bits of work and got paid cash in hand. Then friends who have their own business asked me to do some work with them, but they needed a mechanism for paying me. I set up a limited company and raised an invoice. That's when FM Workplace Services was born. However, a sequence of events put the business on hold.

Kirstie and I went to Dubai for the Easter holidays. A few days into the holiday I got a call from my sister saying the family had been told my dad had very little time left to live. Alex was terrific, and managed to get Kirstie and me on the next flight home from Dubai, but I got another call a few hours later, before we got on the plane to say that dad had passed away. Alex booked himself on the flight after us, and we all came home.

That was the most horrendous flight I have ever been on; despite travelling first class, it seemed to last forever. The only good thing was that I could hide within my own little cabin and no one could see my tears. It was such a waste, all the fantastic food and drink, the amazing service of travelling first class, and I didn't want them to disturb me. I only had a cup of tea and a bit of shortbread during the eight-hour flight. I've made a promise to myself that the next time I travel first class I am going to make sure I enjoy it.

Funeral arrangements were made, and Alex and I went to see my dad. Even now I regret not being able to see him one last time before he passed, not that it would have made a difference. Dad had Alzheimer's and didn't know who we were. During the week we were waiting for the funeral, Alex slipped, and dislocated his shoulder. A trip to the hospital showed that the damage had been done to his shoulder during his many years as a rugby player, and it meant he needed reconstructive surgery. They patched him up enough so that he could get through the next few weeks, and the hospital here let him take all his records so he could be treated in Dubai. When he got back to Dubai, the doctors agreed that he needed surgery, but he postponed it so that he could give my sister away at her wedding in June, in Dad's place.

Immediately after the wedding, Alex and I flew back out to Dubai. We got an overnight flight, and arrived in Dubai at eight o'clock in the morning. We went to the flat, dropped all our luggage, then jumped back in the taxi to the hospital to have his reconstruction surgery. It was supposed to be day surgery but there was a problem because the anaesthetist managed to damage one of the nerves in his arm, which meant he was in hospital for a few days.

Once Alex got out of hospital, I came back to the UK to help Kirstie get organised for going to university. She looked like she was moving into a mansion rather than a tiny room in student halls. My friends who had a Land Rover agreed to drive us down. We got to Durham, helped her unpack, went for something to eat, and then left her to her new life as a student. I climbed into the back seat of the car and cried for most of the journey home to an empty house. Kirstie graduated from Durham in 2017, did a Master's degree in London and has now started work for a gallery in London. I still cry a little bit every time we part after a visit.

I think that was almost worse than when Alex went away. I had been so used to looking after someone, and suddenly there was no one to look after. I had always assumed I'd move to Dubai when Kirstie went to University, that I'd get a job and continue our future. Being ill means that I can't get medical insurance out there, and to pay for my medication and doctor's appointments, etc. is too expensive. I struggled with that, because I never envisaged I would live 4,000 miles away from my husband for such a long time. I still have moments when it's a big deal but with the help of good friends, a counsellor and loads of tissues, I get by.

It was just after Kirstie left, I saw a friend's Facebook post about a charity he was involved with that was looking to move premises. My immediate thought was I wonder if I could help with that – after all, that was my job.

I called them and explained what I was thinking and went in for a chat. Four years on, they still haven't moved, and I'm still volunteering. I love it. I've been a trustee on the board for the last year and half. The Well Multi-Cultural Resource Centre provides help and support for thousands of people every year and holds a special place in my heart. We work with people of different nationalities and cultures and help them with day-to-day issues. That's a significant part of my life. When I made the decision to work for them, I was adamant that nothing was ever going to interfere with that time. I am now on the Board of another organisation that works in Govanhill, and hopefully, I will be able to make a small difference to the people who live there.

Around this time, I remembered I had a limited company, so I decided I would try doing facilities management. One of the problems with facilities management is that it's so broad, so when I went to networking events and had sixty seconds to say what I did, it was difficult to articulate it. I focused on health and safety and started making some money. Through health and safety, I started working with investors and buy-to-let landlords. I would manage the whole refurbishment and get the property ready to go back on the market or be turned into serviced accommodation, or if it was for a landlord, I would prepare it to be sub-let. I loved it, I was back doing what I enjoyed most, but on a smaller scale.

But there was one particular job where I had it all planned, and it was all going like clockwork. I went on holiday for a week. During that time, the people I was working for brought forward the date of the carpet installation by a week, and I needed that week to finish the work. There was so much work to get done, so it meant everybody ended up working really stupid hours. I was onsite for fifteen or sixteen hours a day, and I made myself really ill, and became bedridden for a number of days.

As anyone with fibromyalgia will tell you, it's impossible to work those kinds of hours. I am supposed to pace myself. That made me rethink what I was doing, and I realised that I needed to do something I could do when I felt ok and leave it when I didn't.

I looked at network marketing. I thought that it was a good model for someone with my condition, and I set up a network marketing business. My heart wasn't really in that though. Despite spending a lot of money buying products, and testers for people to try. I knew that it wasn't for me.

But strangely, during that time, I started getting more and more jobs for my first business FM Workplace Services writing policies and procedures for people. I was getting more and more requests and proposals sent to me, and people wanting me to create documents for them. Job after job kept coming in, and I knew it was the perfect thing for me. I've always loved writing and dreamt that one day I would write a book, but here was the ideal opportunity for a new business.

It works, because on the days that the pain is too much or my chronic fatigue goes into overdrive, I don't need to do it. If I want to stay in bed all day because I'm sore or tired, then I can. But one of the things I couldn't get my head around was how I was going to scale it. I was doing a lot of online work gained from freelance sites, where they want you to spend a lot of time on the job but want it for as cheap as they can get it. There are only so many hours in a day, so even writing all of those hours, it was never going to enable me to grow or make enough money to replace my full-time income.

It was either make do with that or do something else. Someone mentioned mentoring people, and that I show them how to set up a solid foundation for their business by using documents as a structured framework. However, building an online business was not something I knew much about. So, I hired coaches to give me the tools I needed to grow my business. I spent a lot of money educating myself and it's working!

My newly branded business, BusiWriter, is beginning to really take off, and I now know that's precisely what I should have been doing all along. I tried to set up my first business without any help, but the difference this time is incredible.

My health continues to get worse. I am in constant pain and on seriously strong drugs. I regularly fall and drop things and pass out occasionally. This is the worst bit of living on my own. I'm scared that one day when I fall and hurt myself, no one will know. I still desperately miss having Alex and Kirstie around, but I have the flexibility and freedom which comes from being self-employed and can visit them both whenever I want. I absolutely love it.

There's one more thing I do as part of my business journey, and that's to tell women in my age group that you can start again.

You can set up a business.

You can be successful.

The definition of success is what you want it to be.

I hope that the journey that I have been on, and the ones I've still to take, are to show people of my age, that it's not all over. It's not just sitting back and making do until you retire. You can keep going. I want to be that example. I want to be the light that says if you're over forty, you can still start and have a successful business. Even illness doesn't need to get in the way unless you let it.

I am 58 years of age and I'm in pain every day of my life. I take loads of medication, but I still work. Some days are harder than others, and some days I can't do anything. I am still the same person as I always was, even when my body lets me down. Yes, there are times when I get angry and frustrated about the things that I don't have, like my health, a regular income, and my husband living in the same country, but I have a fantastic support network of family and friends who are there if I need them.

I would never have believed that day, four years ago, when I left my full-time job, that I'd be where I am today – running a business, collaborating on a book, running a face-to-face networking group for women and being on the board of two organisations.

It's taken me some time to work out what my big 'why' is right now. I'm excluding Alex and Kirstie from that because that's a given, everything I do, is for us. My key objective is to show women my age, that there's as much to life as you want there to be.

Just go out and make your own future, create your own happiness and be an inspiration to others.

ABOUT THE AUTHOR

Joyce spent over 30 years working in the corporate sector, mainly in Financial Services till 2014.

In 2012, she was diagnosed with a chronic medical condition which in the early stages was controlled by medication. In the summer of 2013, she took a viral infection which left her bedridden and unable to do anything for months. In February 2014, after 8 months off work, Joyce parted company with her employers.

In March 2014, as she began to get her strength back, she decided to apply for work. Joyce asked some friends if they knew of anything and was referred to a business not far from where she lived. They wanted someone to draw up some documentation on a freelance basis. Joyce was the perfect fit and when they needed an official business name to pay her, FM Workplace Services was born.

Joyce then briefly joined a MLM company, however, during this time, she noticed that she was getting more and more clients looking for the production of robust business contracts, documents and content. She saw a gap in the market for content and copywriting, then rebranded the FM business and Busiwriter was born.

JOYCE HARDIE
Founder of BusiWriter.
www.busiwriter.co.uk

  @Busiwriter

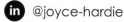 @joyce-hardie

Natasha Leigh Bray

CHAPTER 10
Your Success Starts With You
By Natasha Leigh Bray

"Next level success comes from taking action from a place of true self-belief, self-worth, and self-love."

It was August 2017, and I was sitting in my kitchen holding back the tears and trying to put on a brave face while I fed my ten-month-old baby. I had just become a single mum, and had been signed off from my social work job with stress, and postnatal depression. My business was barely making enough money to pay myself or my part-time staff member the minimum wage.

I had no idea how I was going to turn things around, but it was one of those defining moments in my life. I said to myself, 'Natasha, it's now or never'. I handed in my notice at my social work job and jumped into the unknown with a fierce determination to make things work. Just fifteen months later it paid off as I celebrated becoming a six-figure business owner making six times more than my previous business revenue.

I love making a massive impact on the women I am here to serve. On a daily basis, I get testimonials from women who are experiencing life-changing results through the services I'm offering. That massively boosts your feel-good factor about the work you do, and I quickly realised I was living my life's purpose.

It's incredible, scary and a little unbelievable all at the same time, but if there's one thing I want you to take away from reading my chapter, it's that...your success starts with you.

Let me introduce myself. I'm Natasha, a Psychology Expert and Rapid Transformation Coach for women, and mum to my beautiful miracle son, Jenson. My mission in life is not only to be the best mum I can, but also to help women create a remarkable transformation in their lives and businesses.

My business began in the health industry but has quickly expanded into helping women unlock their success mindset to rapidly grow their own businesses. They might sound like two very different areas, but in fact, they are both influenced by the same underlying triggers and beliefs. I will tell you more about that later.

I am so proud of what I have achieved, but I want to be very clear, success wasn't always available to me, and that makes me even more grateful. I am sharing my journey with you because it could make a difference, and help you to unlock your own success.

There will be tears.
There will be disbelief.
There will be shock.

But most of all, there will be advice, lessons, and hopefully, inspiration that could take you from feeling stuck to unstoppable in your business too.

My business journey began in 2014 with a dream and a white feather. I had a dream that I was making peanut butter and found a white feather in my car the next morning. I was going through a spiritual awakening at the time, and I took it as a sign that I was meant to start my food business, Naturally Guilt Free. I had several food intolerances and was always on a 'diet' and so started making my own gluten, dairy and sugar-free treats to sell while I was completing my Masters in Social Work.

Nobody knew I was secretly battling bulimia.

I was very controlling over my food, addicted to exercise, and used laxatives to purge food from my body. Nobody guessed because I looked healthy and fit.

Eventually, it started to take its toll on me.

My hair started falling out, and I ended up with adrenal fatigue and heart palpitations. I also severely injured my back in the gym. After a year of trying to get pregnant, I was sent for fertility investigations. The tests came back 'inconclusive', and I was told it was unexplained infertility. I knew my body was shutting down on me. I desperately wanted to be a mum, so this was the wake-up call I needed.

How had I let it get this bad?

My childhood wasn't easy. It has taken a lot of self-development, self-love, and strength for me to become the woman I am now. I grew up in a small town called Bridgend in South Wales. I went through long-term abuse and bullying throughout my childhood, which is something I have now forgiven but will never forget.

I was bullied relentlessly because I was overweight. I was the 'fat kid' at school. I also wore glasses, came from a council estate and had braces, all the little things children pick out as being different and a reason to bully you for.

I had no confidence whatsoever, absolutely none.

I was so shy I wouldn't even walk past someone in the street. I would cross the road on purpose so that I didn't have to walk past them. I'd just stare at the floor. That's how little confidence I had.

Looking back, I think food became a coping mechanism for me.

Sadly, lots of women who suffer child abuse will use weight as a shield. I thought gaining weight could protect me in some way. Food became the only thing I had to turn to, essentially.

Going through abuse as a child is a living nightmare. I spoke out about the abuse at several points throughout my life, but I wasn't believed. That was one of the most hurtful things I had to come to terms with. I had nobody to turn to. Nobody to protect me. No escape.

I would go as far as saying that not being believed was more damaging and long-lasting to me than the abuse itself.

I started gaining a lot of weight from about the age of ten, so I started secondary school overweight – a UK size sixteen, which is not large by any means, but being a young child, you stand out.

I didn't have many friends at all, and I found it very difficult to actually keep friends too. When I did have a group of people around me, I was always the one who was bullied within it for some reason.

I never realised the lasting impact it would have on me.

Then when it came to me being visible in my business, I started having issues with putting myself out there. I knew it stemmed back to when I was bullied, a time when I was made to feel like I never had anything significant to say.

I've worked so hard to overcome this fear and to be brave and visible in my business.

I started going on nights-out when I was about fifteen. I then began drinking, which became a bit of a replacement for food really. It numbed the pain and the things I didn't want to deal with.

I started to lose weight from about sixteen onward. I was so lost. My reason for wanting to lose weight was to find a man who could 'rescue' me. I believed I needed to be slim to be loved.

I was so desperate to feel loved and safe.

That's when my toxic relationship with food and exercise began. I started losing weight in unhealthy ways, exercising for five hours at a time, eating half meals, and taking laxatives and diet pills. This went on for a really long time.

I went from one extreme to another – overweight for my age to a very slim, size six. I became very controlled with food and exercise as a way of coping.

As I already mentioned, I caused a lot of damage to my body. That's why I'm so passionate now about helping women lose weight in safe ways.

It was a huge confidence boost when I lost weight, and the boys who used to bully me at school tried to hit on me, not knowing I was the girl they had been at school with for five years. I looked so different. Nobody knew I was Natasha Bray, the 'fat girl' from school. They didn't even recognise me.

I was still very, very shy. I knew I was physically smaller but a big part of my mind always thought I was fat. Even though I was buying size six clothes, I was telling myself, 'Oh, you're not really that size. It's just the clothes in this shop are big sizes.' I still believed I needed to lose more weight. I had a very unhealthy perception of myself. Most of my confidence came from the confidence boost alcohol gives you, rather than having inner confidence.

I think I've blocked out a lot of my younger years, and in some ways, my uni years as well. I started going out drinking around five nights a week by that point. I didn't do my best at University. I missed a lot of the classes and was hungover most of the time. I also didn't really respect myself and went out with guys who weren't nice guys.

I had no self-worth and was looking for love in all the wrong places.

I remember being in an on-off relationship with one particular guy. It was a very toxic. We had a big argument one night when I discovered he'd been texting another woman. That argument ended in him actually strangling me. His friend walked in and stopped him. I couldn't get him off me, and I think, if his friend hadn't walked in, I wouldn't be here today.

Afterwards, I just cried hysterically. The next morning, when I looked in the mirror, I was horrified to see all the bruising and burst blood vessels in my eyes, from all the force and pressure. I realised then that he had strangled me for quite some time.

Looking back, I put up with so much more than I should have. I was always trying to make him love me because I didn't love myself. Afterwards, like a lot of women do, I felt like the assault was my fault because I started the argument. He actually told me he was suicidal, and because I felt such overwhelming guilt, I didn't even report what he did to me. I thought that if I went to the police, I'd be responsible for ruining someone's life. That's how I felt back then.

I also had to make a tough decision when I had an abortion in the early stages of pregnancy with his child. The guilt and shame of having the abortion affected me more than the attack itself. I had always wanted children, and it affected me profoundly.

My issues with bulimia and exercise addiction were the key influences for what I do now. I've worked with so many women going through difficulties or holding themselves back because of shame. That's why I am sharing this.

I may be judged yes, but I may also help set someone else free.

When you own your story, you can no longer be judged or shamed – it sets you free.

This experience of the attack and the abortion also became my biggest driver. I had to turn it into something positive. It was the only way I could cope with the pain. I honestly believe it's the main contributing factor to where I am today. I wrote a poem to always remember the life I lost:

The hardest thing was letting you go.
The saddest thing is you, I will never know.
I made a promise it wouldn't be in vain.
Thanks for making me who I am today.

He has been in touch with me since it all happened. It was a long time ago now. He apologised and said it's one of the biggest regrets of his life. I've let go of anything to do with that now. I think the best way to overcome struggles in life is to turn them into something positive. It's not the experience you go through that affects you, it's the meaning you place on that experience. That experience obviously affected me for a while, and then I thought, 'How can I turn this into something positive? Why has this happened to me?'

As a result, I ended up changing my degree to something I was more passionate about, and that was psychology.

I told myself I was going to make something of my life. All this disrespecting myself, being with bad boys and men who didn't respect me, had to stop. All the drinking until I blacked out had to stop. I gave my all to my degree, and graduated with the accolade of best-performing student and won two awards for my work.

The attack changed my life, but I had the choice to let it change me for the worse, or for the better.

This may be hard for some to understand but I truly forgive him. Holding hate or anger inside only hurts us. I forgave him long before I ever forgave myself.

Isn't it funny how we are our own biggest bullies sometimes?

Many women who come to me struggling to lose weight, or take action in their businesses, have forgiveness work to do. Most often it's forgiveness for themselves and letting go of the guilt that's literally eating away at them. This quote really sums it up:

'To forgive is to set the prisoner free, and discover that the prisoner was you.'

So, how did I get where I am now? Well after that traumatic time in my life I started working with a charity, for homelessness services, in victim support. And then I secured a job with a homeless organisation, working specifically with the most complex clients who have mental health issues as well as drug or alcohol addiction. It was intense, but I loved the work.

After that, I decided to get more qualifications in addiction studies and a Master's in Social Work too. I was addicted to growing and learning. Alongside this, my health was deteriorating. As I said before, I was told I had unexplained infertility. I thought I was being punished and it was a huge wake-up call. I started researching how to heal my body naturally alongside running my health food business.

I found that lots of women suffer from autoimmune conditions, which are exacerbated by stress. I knew that I had to get to work on myself and begin to be kind to my mind and body. I asked myself daily questions like, 'Why did I feel I needed to do all this exercise?' and 'Why couldn't I just accept my body?' I was very, very fit and slim and lean because I had some muscle from all the exercise I was doing, but I still didn't think it was good enough; and that's when I asked myself, 'What is the true issue here?' That's when I started working on self-love and self-acceptance.

One big lesson I learned was that my problems with food and obsession with my weight were never because of the food itself. They were due to deeper issues around my self-worth that needed to be healed.

I did a lot of conscious work on loving myself, which did have an impact. Although I weighed more, I looked healthier. I had to stop weighing myself ten times a day and realise my self-worth was not based on my weight on the scales.

It wasn't a quick journey.

There was a lot of trial and error.

I was successful at losing weight, but not always in a safe way. I had to learn a new way – one that healed my body. A big part of what I do on the health side of my business is taking that trial and error away from women. I now know what works, and what works quickly, if you want to lose weight healthily and safely. Women on my programmes eat more food than they've ever eaten before yet still lose weight, which baffles them at first. They're very fixated on the scales, which I understand. It's something that's been drummed into us. People often think they need to eat less to lose weight, when that's not the case.

I healed my infertility through the power of nutrition and a holistic approach to my health. My beautiful little boy came along unexpectedly, while I was working in a specialist addiction social worker team. A very welcome surprise. I can't describe how much it meant to me, to have my dream of becoming a mum fulfilled. I was still addicted to exercise at this point in my life, but I was fuelling my body correctly and followed a pregnancy-safe exercise programme.

Unfortunately, I had a very traumatic birth with my son, and the doctors told me I would never be able to lift weights or do high impact exercise again. This is what spiralled me into postnatal depression. Exercise was such a huge part of my life. Once that was taken from me, I was forced to look at my self-worth issues on a deeper level to help my recovery.

At this same time, I was trying to grow my business, so I didn't have to return to work. I was doing 'all the things' to grow my business and really felt like I was on the brink of success.

But something was stopping me. It took me a while, but I finally figured it out.

ME. I WAS GETTING IN MY OWN WAY.

I saw the same thing happening with my health clients. They knew how to eat healthily, how to exercise, and how to lose weight. But they were not doing it. Something was holding them back, or they sabotaged their efforts when they started to feel good or achieve success.

Another valuable lesson: Success is eighty per cent mindset, twenty per cent strategy.

You've probably heard the quote, 'knowledge is power', right? This used to be one of my favourite quotes, until recently. But knowledge is only power if you take action on it. And this is where most people struggle. Because IF we take action in our business, it's not determined by the knowledge we have.

It's determined by our MINDSET: our thoughts, our beliefs about ourselves, our fears, and our doubts. HOW we take action is also determined by our mindset.

I often find that our goals are in conflict with our inner beliefs. And it's this conflict, caused by our mindset, that stops us achieving the success we want.

When I found out about Rapid Transformation Therapy, I knew it was the missing piece to get my clients the results they needed and deserved. I already had fantastic results with my clients, but there were lots of women who kept self-sabotaging. Quite often they knew what they needed to do, but something stopped them doing it. It's the deep-rooted subconscious beliefs that are actually preventing them from moving forward and achieving the goals. When your subconscious beliefs conflict with your conscious goals and desires, that's when we hit resistance or self-sabotage.

Rapid Transformational Therapy was an absolute GAME CHANGER for me, and not just for my business but personally too.

Rapid Transformational Therapy is a revolutionary new super-therapy that mixes hypnosis, CBT, NLP and other forms of therapy into one package. It works in as little as one session by accessing the deep subconscious beliefs and memories you don't even realise are still impacting on you today. In thirteen years of working in behaviour-change psychology using various tools and techniques, I have never witnessed or experienced anything as powerful as this therapy. I use it in my own unique way, mixed with my many years of working in psychology and therapy to get incredible results for my clients.

I will never forget my very first rapid transformation client. She had been binge-eating thirty pounds of junk food on a daily basis for over twenty-five years. She would eat to the point where she was physically sick and then do it all over again the next day. Within twenty-eight days of working with me using a mix of Rapid Transformational Therapy and coaching, her binge-eating had stopped. How? We dug deep into finding the root cause using Rapid Transformational Therapy.

What we discovered was, in fact, she never felt loved as a child. And as soon as she realised it was just a coping mechanism to feel more loved throughout the years, I was able to help her see that she was actually loved as a child, it just wasn't in the way that she needed to be shown love, and it set her free. Her attempts at weight loss have been more successful now, and she even ran a half marathon recently.

I've cured clients of cocaine addiction, depression, comfort eating, emotional eating, sugar addiction, and various other health issues. My favourite packages though are the ones where I get to help heal women's self-worth and self-love, to help them become more successful in their business. I know this one from experience.

Experiencing the therapy for myself helped me access what was impacting my self-worth on a deep subconscious level, and allowed me to rewire my beliefs to powerful ones, and heal my lack of self-love and self-worth.

The effect was nothing short of profound.

That very same month my business revenue skyrocketed to thousands of pounds more than it had ever been before. I wondered if it was a coincidence or a fluke.

The next month it went thousands higher than that again, over four times more than it had been that same month the year before. Then it kept rising! I had a couple more Rapid Transformational Therapy sessions during this time for various issues, and I went from 3.5k months at the start of 2018 to 22k months by November 2018. Not only that, but my results with my clients dramatically boosted too, and I was getting incredible messages and testimonials on a daily basis. I was fully booked with clients months in advance even though my prices had tripled. I became an Amazon bestselling co-author, featured in the local and national press and began to get recognised as an expert.

I realised something. I had found the key to unlocking true success mindset. This taught me a valuable lesson about success: next level success, rapid success, incredible success...happens when you take action, but that cannot be achieved with regular mindset work alone. You must combine it with the deeper subconscious work RTT offers. It makes sense, right? How can you reach your full potential if you don't believe you can have it or deserve it?

Not only did I get phenomenal results in my own business, but people started coming to me for success in their own business too. One client came to me for help with a better work-life balance. She was a classic people-pleaser (sign of low self-love), offering discounts, and not charging her worth, not following up on invoices owed to her. When we finished her twenty-eight-day package and looked at her results, she had received over £17,000 in chased up unpaid invoices and was no longer letting people take advantage of her. Her staff had started to respect her more too, due to this new shift in her.

Another client feared being visible in the online space, and it was really holding her back in her business. I discovered she had a fear of being judged and fear of success, deep-rooted from childhood. So, we went back to the memories, healed them and rewired the beliefs that stemmed from them. She more than doubled her usual income that same month and became super comfortable with being very visible in her business.

I will never forget my first business success client. She added £4000 extra to her monthly revenue within months of us working together. The funny thing is I did not work on money or business strategies with any of these ladies. I worked on healing their deeper issues around self-love, self-worth and self-belief, which was what actually led to the big jump in their income.

Why? Because what you believe, you attract.

If you believe you are worthless, you won't reach your full earning potential.

What most people don't realise is that your business is a reflection of you.

I've made it my mission now to help as many women as possible unlock their success mindset, and to achieve more success in their business too. I am passionate about helping women become more financially independent and secure on their terms so they can make big impact and big income, around their families.

To reach more women, I mixed RTT with business strategy and mindset work into a knock-out online course, The Success Accelerator.

The launch was a huge hit, making £34,000 in its debut! That was my yearly wage as a social worker, and I made it in one month! The transformations for these women have been incredible. I actually celebrated by treating myself to a new cooking pan set. I'm really not materialistic, and for me, it's just about building a financially secure future for myself and my family. I have my home, and a car that gets me from A to B, and I have my son and a wonderful partner. That's really all I need. My dream would be to be mortgage-free, so that's what I am going to aim for over the next five years.

I'm so excited for what the future holds, not just for my business but for all the women I get to impact along the way. The belief 'I am enough' changes every area of your life – it's like a ripple effect. There is nothing more uplifting than supporting women to create this huge change in their lives.

The next stage for me is to scale my business even further through my online programmes and to reach more women. I am also currently writing my own book to spread my message further to the women who need to hear it.

What started as a dream and a white feather has turned into far more than I could ever have imagined.

I want to tell you who are reading this today, that your success starts with you!

Take action on the things in your heart that you want to achieve in your life. Maybe you're thinking, 'I'm not good enough to do that.' Perhaps you've got those past blocks from things from your childhood or an abusive relationship. Maybe you're holding yourself back in your business, and you don't know why.

Please know that you are enough. You are more than enough, and you always have been, regardless of your past. You are more than worthy of all forms of abundance in your life: success, love, money, health, and happiness.

All you need to do is believe.

ABOUT THE AUTHOR

Natasha Bray lives in Bridgend, South Wales, with her son Jenson. A best-selling author, Rapid Transformation Coach and Psychology Expert, her passion is empowering busy women who want to take their power back, learn to love and believe in themselves and experience rapid transformation in their health and business.

After healing from years of low self-worth, eating disorders and food addiction and exercise addition, she established her business Guilt Free Health in 2014, making it her mission to help women heal the root cause of their health, confidence and weight issues so they could achieve their goals safely.

In early 2018 she expanded into helping women with their success in business after achieving her own success through 4 key areas of mindset work. She has a unique background in Psychology, Addictions, Social work, Nutrition and Rapid Transformational Therapy which she combines in her services to get rapid, life changing results with her clients.

NATASHA LEIGH BRAY

Best-selling author, Rapid Transformation Coach and Psychology Expert.
www.natashabray.co.uk

Rapid Transformation Coach, Guilt Free Health
www.guiltfreehealth.com

Bridget Zyka

CHAPTER 11
My journey to allowing myself to just be and listen to my body!
By Bridget Zyka

"Be yourself. Everyone else is already taken."
– Oscar Wilde

I can remember being a really outdoorsy child. I grew up on a farm in the middle of nowhere in Ireland, five miles to the nearest town. You needed a car to go everywhere in this kind of place. There was no such thing as public transport, it simply didn't exist. Even now, it doesn't really exist.

I was outside every chance I had. I'd pull on a pair of wellies, go out the door, and then I was gone. I would be gone all day. I wouldn't tell my parents where I was and I can remember it used to drive them mad, but I just loved the freedom of being on my own and exploring; I suppose that's never really left me. My favourite place was down by the river. Hanging upside down out of trees just doing all kinds of silly, tomboyish things.

My earliest memory, I think, is being about two and a half and taking tea in a glass bottle and sandwiches down to my dad, who was working away down the fields somewhere. I took my dog with me for company, and my mum tried to follow me. I kept telling her to just go back to the house, I was fine. Fierce independence, even at the age of two... When I reflect, I think my entire life has been shaped by the way I was a child!

I used to run away all the time. At only two or three, I'd run up the lane to my neighbour's house all the time. At the top of our lane there was some barbed wire, and my mum remembers me lying on my belly, rolling underneath, putting the wire back up, and running up to my neighbour's house. I was always up to mischief when I was a kid. I wasn't very controllable let's just say.

I have always been really close to my dad. I was Daddy's girl, really. Every chance I had, I was with my dad. My earliest memory is of him throwing me in the back of the car with all my teddies, and going down to our local creamery. This was before school started. I remember changing into my clothes for school in the car because I was still in my pyjamas. He'd just throw me in with my clothes, and I'd get ready on the way, and then when we'd got back home and I'd go off to school. We used to do that quite regularly, and on the weekend when I was a teenager, my dad and I would just take off for a drive. He actually taught me how to drive, and would take me down all these roads and places I'd never been just to show me where they were and to get experience. Because of where we lived, you needed a car to go anywhere, so learning to drive was essential.

We also went to GAA (Gaelic football) games together. We were never far apart. Thick as thieves the whole time, and I always used to back him up and cover for him, if needed. I miss those simple times a lot now in this fast-paced city I live in!

Primary school was a magical time. There were only seven in my class. I was quite creative and into painting, and we used to take potatoes into school and cut shapes into them. Then we'd dab them into paint and print the shapes onto paper; I remember we used to spend hours and hours painting, colouring-in, and making stuff. I used to knit and crochet too. I still do bits of creative stuff every so often, but I was quite creative back then, I think. I was trying to express myself as much as I could, because I was quite loud, and always wanted to be seen.

History was one of my favourite subjects in secondary school. I was always reading ahead in history. I was fascinated by what happened hundreds of years ago, and used to try to go as far back as I could to find out as much as possible. I was always skipping ahead in subjects. I remember being in French class and getting into trouble, because the teacher had asked me a question, but I wasn't paying attention. I'd answer the question and then go back to talking to my friends and messing about. I was clever, but I was probably too smart for my own good. I wasn't stimulated, so I was trying to skip ahead, and that was my way of trying to keep myself interested in what I was doing.

I'm from Cavan in the midlands. It's about an hour and a half, two hours north-west of Dublin, where there's not too much happening, so making your own adventures was a necessity. Usually, everybody ends up in Dublin at some point in their life, either for college, university or sometimes for work. The goal when you're growing up, is to get out of where you're from, and go to the capital city or to the nearest big town. I was driven to be different when I was a kid. I was always pushing my boundaries. I was a real rebel as a teenager, I did all kinds of stupid stuff.

Before I went to uni, I got really ill. I had glandular fever, and it was truly awful. The thing about having something like glandular fever is it comes back again and again if you don't look after yourself. It's triggered by stressful events in your life. I've also had adrenal fatigue in the last few years. When I developed glandular fever, I was at risk of developing chronic fatigue syndrome. I was pushing myself far too much, and it was my body's way of saying slow down. I was working in a local supermarket and also doing some admin IT work over the summer, trying to make money to go to university and I wasn't eating properly either.

I got a rash, all over me, which is one of the main symptoms. My mother was a nurse, so she knew there was something wrong straight away. She took me to the doctor, and I had to go to casualty. I then got admitted because I started to faint and feel sick in the bathroom while I was waiting. I ended up in hospital for a week and I was told not to go to university by my doctor, and of course, me being me, I said...'I'm going anyway' ... and I went anyway.

University didn't go completely to plan. I failed one subject, then had to move to a different university and try again. I had to try a couple of times, but I got through in the end. I got my degree and two other qualifications as well. I've always tried to justify what I can do, and express my creativity as best I can. I think we are a little mean to ourselves sometimes as we don't always feel like we're enough, and we feel that we need to justify our decisions for being different and not following a set path.

When you're older, it's important to keep your health strong and eat healthy food, instead of the processed stuff we all reach for. I tend to reach for the sugar and coffee when I'm tired. It's typical in IT culture, and other corporate roles, to survive on coffee and sugary snacks, but when you're older it comes back to bite you on the bum when you least expect it! I now try to eat as healthily as I can and take a range of supplements too. I also pay attention to my body, and if I'm not feeling one-hundred percent, I'll take action sooner, for example, resting more instead of feeling I should push myself.

After college and university, I worked for about two years, and then went to Canada, came back home and worked for a while, and then went to Australia, and then onto New Zealand, where I lived for six years. I essentially travelled as much as I could over the course of ten years.

I moved to London just over two years ago and while here, I met my husband within three months, which scuppered my plan for going to South America. So now I'm based in London for the foreseeable future.

Australia was really tough because you only get a one-year working holiday visa, and you're only allowed to work for six months at a time for one employer. They also don't really like backpackers to start with anyway. They don't want to hire anyone who can only work for six months for them. I stayed in Melbourne for a few weeks, and then I went to Sydney where my cousin lived. I had the option of staying there rent-free and finding a job and all the rest of it, but I only stayed for a few weeks, because otherwise I wouldn't have got to see any of Australia. I didn't want to get sucked up into the whole Irish and Sydney thing. It just revolves around drinking and all the rest of it, and I didn't want to do that. I wanted to do something different, and stand on my own two feet.

So, I left, and I went travelling up the coast, and I ended up living in Cairns, very far north in Queensland. I was there for about four or five months in total, working all kind of jobs. I was a graphic designer, and ran a hostel. I was even doing pub crawls, getting people to go out and get drunk, and organising lots of events for backpackers. But, after a few months, I'd had enough. I needed to get a proper job, so I moved down to Brisbane. I spent two days travelling by car with my friends. We camped out on the side of the road. I ended up in Brisbane and got a job in IT for a few months. The main thing I learned whilst living there was that I can be very resourceful when I need to be. I learned to dig deep and decide what was important.

I had enough money from that to move to New Zealand. I got a job within a week of arriving, but it took me a long time to adjust because the weather was much colder, similar to Ireland. I love the sun, even though I'm Irish and it took me about six months to adjust. For most of that time I was wearing leggings underneath my clothes because I was so cold. New Zealand's a great country and everything, but it's very far away, and you can plateau in your career after a few years. It's a lovely place to be, but family and commitment kind of take priority after a number of years. You have to make a decision. My heart was saying, 'What do you really want to do?' and my head was thinking, 'what's the sensible option?' London was my kind of compromise. I'm still close enough to be at home if I need to be at home for a reason, but I'm still far enough away that I have independence and my own life.

I was slightly worried at first about travelling so much on my own, but I realised I have a real gift for making friends easily. I can click with people straight away and be best friends for life, and it happens when you travel all the time.

When you're travelling in foreign places, things like going to the bathroom, become a bit of a hassle, because when you've got loads of bags to look after, you're paranoid someone's going to rob your stuff if you fall asleep. You get so worried, but it's what you do. It makes you stronger. When I was younger, everyone was saying: don't go travelling, wait until you get a boyfriend, wait until you do this, and wait until such and such. I knew if I waited it would never happen. You need to go when the moment strikes.

I did actually have a boyfriend at the time, but that didn't really work out. I had a friend I wanted to go travelling with, and that didn't really work out either, so I was like, you know what, I'm going to go on my own anyway. I'm not waiting for you, not waiting for somebody else, I'm going to go. I wanted to go, so I went.

Some of my best memories of travelling were when I hired a bike in San Francisco and cycled across the Golden Gate Bridge, and then I went all the way to Sausalito and took the ferry back. I didn't go to Alcatraz like everyone else. I usually try and do different things. I went to the Mission District and hung out with people. In New York, I was in a shop, I think it was Lower East Side, and I got talking to some girl, and then she invited me to go out with her and her friend. We went bowling at midnight in New York. Going to the top of the Empire State Building was amazing too as was doing the Great Wall of China on my own, and passing through its twenty-two watchtowers. I don't speak a word of Chinese, and I was in Beijing on my own with Mandarin written down on pieces of card, getting taxis on my own, smiling and nodding, and trying to explain where I was going. Just doing crazy stuff. I once got on a bus in Laos, and had a kid beside me who was sick the whole way.

When I was in Thailand, I was the only westerner living in the area I was in. I'd jump on the local minibus to go to the Tesco, because it was the only western experience I could get, or I'd go to a coffee shop which had all the magazines in foreign languages.

I tried to get into my own routine. Wherever I lived in the world, I would always try and find a coffee shop or somewhere I could just go and relax and chill out and forget about stuff for a while. I'd read a magazine or a book and get lost for a while, forget about any problems or whatever was going on. Not always problems, but just to tune out for a while, and take a break, and then figure out my next plan.

Vietnam is another great travel memory. I spent lots of time on the beach, going out clubbing and swimming at midnight, and because I was paranoid about having my things stolen when I went swimming, I used to hide them under a boat on the beach. My friends always said I should have written a blog or written books about travelling, I have so many stories.

I uncovered so much about myself through travelling...for a start, I'm super independent and quite stubborn when I want to be. I like my freedom, but I guess it's a decision you make. Everyone questions you when you're travelling on your own. 'Why aren't you married? Are you a lesbian? What's wrong with you? Grow up. Buy a house.' You feel pressured to do all this stuff, but when you're older, you still have plenty of time. There's a whole timeline that people give you as a woman, as a man as well, but women get it worse from society. When you're travelling on your own and you're getting all these questions like, 'Where's your husband? Why don't you have a husband? What's wrong with you? Don't you like men?' They'd ask you all these silly things that they'd never ask a man. It's just ridiculous. I used to make up a boyfriend so they'd leave me alone.

People are just a bit closed-minded sometimes about it, but all people are different. We're all different for a reason, but my decision to go travelling was essential to me. Now I'm older, I don't feel the need to travel like when I was younger. I got it out of my system. I've seen the most incredible places. Before London was fully integrated into my life, I decided to go travelling to India, Paris, Spain, Portugal, and Amsterdam, to name but a few. It was like the last hurrah before the serious and sensible side could take over again.

I still like to travel, but I want a bit more luxury these days. I can now afford to have a nice hotel and not a crappy backpack place that's ten to twenty people in a dorm room. You know? I've done that. I suppose it takes a different type of person to put up with doing that, and not knowing what you're going to do. You're in beautiful places, but you've nobody to share it with. You're looking at these amazing sunsets and in very romantic places, but you're on your own. Despite that, I found strength in being alone, and I knew that if I was meant to meet somebody, I'd meet them. There's somebody out there for all of us, after all.

I had no intention of meeting someone when I came to London. My plan was to go to South America after a year or two and then to move again, but when I was in New Zealand, I had planned to go to Japan, but I decided not to, because I didn't want to start from scratch four years in a row. I wanted to stay and make roots for a while, so I did that for six years. I then moved to London, which has probably been one of the toughest places to live for me. I've almost adjusted now, but it's taken me a fair amount of time to figure out how this place works. I had to ease myself into coming to London for sure.

I took my time coming to London as I knew an extended period of travel probably wouldn't happen for a while. I came initially to study a special effects course because I trained as a makeup artist in New Zealand. I was a personal stylist for a little bit over there as well. I worked on lots of film sets. That was initially what I came here for. It was a pretty steep learning curve because I'm used to people being open and friendly.

The people I ended up making friends with in England were very flakey, and not dependable. Even people I was friends with before I arrived in London weren't very reliable either. I had to rely on myself. I found myself having to adapt to a new way of living again. While I was trying to find a house, I ended up staying with a friend for a week or two, and then I finally found somewhere in Camden. It was absolutely awful. I paid a lot of money to live there, but it had no central heating or living room, and the kitchen was tiny. As you can imagine, I stayed there for only a short while, and then moved again.

London's expensive, so I did what I had to do, and got on with it. You make your own luck! My joke was always, 'I didn't get my dream career, but I got a husband out of it.' Life's what you make it, isn't it? Life's what happens when you're busy making plans.

So, let me tell you how I met my husband! We were out and about one night in Covent Garden at a bar and started chatting, and we hit it off instantly. After that we met up and went for dinner, and then to a pub, and believe it or not we got chucked out because we were kissing too much.

It was an instant thing, and we've never looked back since. He's the only person I've ever felt like that about. We had to be together all of the time, and even though we lived so far apart from each other, we still made a point of seeing each other nearly every other day at least. We kept going even when times got hard, and we survived. We've been married over a year. It hasn't been all a bed of roses, but things are sent to test you, which make you stronger as a couple and as people. We're very independent people as well. We're very strong-minded in our opinions. We work hard at keeping our relationship strong and are both open and honest with each other. We also respect each other's views and give one another space when needed.

The relationship I was in before I met my husband, was quite a bad one... Well, it wasn't very long, but it ended quite badly. He'd lost loads of weight, and because he'd lost weight, he thought that I should too. He'd say things like, 'You'd be so much hotter if you lost thirty kilos' and other similar backhanded, flippant remarks. He knew how to get to me and hurt me. Bullying tactics. I know people who have been in relationships for ten years, and their partners have made them feel so crap about themselves, to the point that they thought they couldn't find anybody else. They convince you that they are the best person you can get, and belittle your confidence, so you feel totally dependent on them, afraid to even go outside the house and do simple things.

I'm generally a confident person, but weight had been an issue in the past, and he seemed to enjoy tapping into those insecurities. He thought he could say what he wanted to me, and that I'd never react.

When I was in New Zealand, my confidence around weight wasn't the best because I was much bigger then. I wasn't in a happy place there either. I was going through lots of stuff, and I wasn't satisfied in my career and wanted something better.

All I wanted to be was happy, and to follow my bliss. I wanted to work for myself and was trying to figure out what the hell I could do, delving into what I am good at, and what comes easily to me. I've always been good with people, and find it easy to relate to people, and connect with them. People have always been able to open up to me and tell me their problems or issues. I'm also quite intuitive, and have been from a young age.

When I was younger and watching TV with my mum or my dad, I used to say what was going to happen all the time. They said, 'You should be a scriptwriter.' It was just a natural talent I had when I was a kid. I never realised what it was called until recently. Synchronicity would happen too. I probably should have died a couple of times, but I was saved because certain things happened. I got out of the way just in time before something happened. I had a few scary moments when I was travelling, but I was always safe at the end of it. There's definitely somebody looking out for me and keeping me safe.

There has been so many moments that I've known intuitively that all would be OK, when my gut-feeling kicked in. You must have felt that? Almost like a sixth sense? Once it happened before I came to London. I had been travelling for three months. I had a bit of a break because I knew I was going into this new career, new city, all the rest of it, so I wanted some time to enjoy myself before I had to be a grown-up again for a while. I was in Paris just before the terrorist attack happened at the concert venue. I was supposed to stay in Paris the day of the event, pretty close to where the venue was, and I was like, 'Oh yeah, I'm going to book a ticket, I'm going to go tomorrow.' Then all of a sudden I got this thing saying, 'No, you're going today.' I was like, 'I don't want to go today.' And then, 'No, you're going today.' This thing kept telling me I had to go and I had to leave now. So I booked the ticket, and I got one of the last flights out of Paris the night before. The next day the devastating terrorist attack happened. All the borders got sealed for a week. I wouldn't have been allowed to leave for over a week, even if I was safe.

Then there was the night I flew from Paris to Madrid to stay with my friend, and the flight got delayed. I was delayed by about six hours getting to my friend's place. I had to take the Metro, and my phone ran out of battery. I couldn't get hold of my friend, and my friend had no clue where I was. In the Metro, I begged the attendant for a charger in my broken Spanish. She luckily had one, and so I charged up my phone and rang my friend. I asked him for directions, and got my Google Maps working. And then my phone died again outside the Metro. I found a pizza place open at one o'clock in the morning, I'd been travelling for at least half a day. The flight should only have taken an hour or two, but these things happen. This waiter let me charge my phone again, and helped me to figure out how to get to my friend's house. I walked up to my friend's house finally, about two o'clock in the morning. I would have been totally screwed. That was the Madrid story.

On the same trip, I went to Granada on the overnight bus from Madrid. I then got on the local bus in Granada to where I was staying. I was trying to ask the bus driver in my broken Spanish how to get to my hotel. Out of nowhere a Canadian guy pops up in the bus and goes, 'Oh, I know where that place is. I can walk you there.' He got off at the bus stop with me and went out of his way to show me where my hotel was. I went there and waited outside for two hours until the hotel opened up. And then at seven o'clock in the morning, I thought I'd go and see when there was a bus to The Alhambra, and there was one already there waiting for me! I loved The Alhambra, it was an amazing experience.

I've had so many moments of synchronicity happen to me. Even yesterday, when I was running around London, looking for a day job. Buses only go every so often when you're in a hurry. All the buses lined up for me yesterday, they were literally there waiting at the bus stops when I needed them. The lights were all on green too. And then on the tube, everything went smoothly,

Everything just works out for me when I'm happy and I get myself into flow, when I'm being positive, and I'm doing things that light me up. This is what I tell women to do, to do things that light you up and make you happy. When you're positive, good things happen for you. It's all tied into the Law of Attraction.

Over the last few years, I've really tried to bring all of my experiences together in a way to inspire and help others too! My business came from talking to a coach friend about what my passion was, and I was talking about how women are treated in society.

When I was a makeup artist, for example, I saw how badly women get treated. Models felt inadequate about their bodies. The pressure they would be under to be absolutely perfect in every way. The thing is, it doesn't matter about your size, it's all about what's inside your head because that's your worst inner critic. Body dysmorphia exists because of the media and marketing campaigns telling us to take a pill and you'll lose ten kilos in a day. We've all been bombarded with that kind of stuff.

Eventually, in September last year, I started a twenty-one-day Facebook group challenge. I did a Facebook Live into the group every single day, and posted actions along with motivational stuff and various quotes. As a result of this, people approached me asking me to give master classes and interviews in their groups. People started asking me how to be confident, and how to love yourself and your body. It was mostly women feeling bad about themselves, not knowing how to ask for help, and not knowing how to get their life on track.

It's taken me a year to get to the point where I'm now being asked to feature on podcasts, and to do media features and be interviewed by some amazing female empowerment platforms. Looking at all these other streams, it sounds like I have arrived here easily, but it's not easy working for yourself. You have to be kind to yourself and keep going and persevering, despite everybody telling you you're crazy every single day. But, if you know your idea has legs, and it's gonna help other women, and give back, then it's worth doing. That's my other thing, I want to give back to other women because I don't want them to have to go through what I went through, or what other women have gone through.

It's not easy to be a woman in today's society because you feel like you have to act like the 1950s perfect housewife and have the job, the career, the kids, the house, the car, to be successful in today's society. We're not allowed to just be — and my mantra for that is, 'just listen to your body', because if you listen to your body, it usually has all the answers. Sometimes we just need to relax, and calm ourselves down, and get into nature, even for five minutes every day: in the local park, or in the sunshine, or just taking a moment to breathe and figure out what's going on with your life, instead of constantly keeping going.

You don't have to do what society expects of you.

It doesn't make you a failure.

You can be your own person.

You are enough.

A lot of problems stem from people not feeling like they're enough, like they have to over-deliver to feel self-worth.

It's time to not care what other people think of you. You just have to grow a thick skin and do it anyway. It's their problem, not yours. It's never about you. It's always about them; people project their fears and weaknesses onto you, and they belittle you to make themselves feel better; it's just the way that some people work. It's hard not to take things personally. After a number of years of people saying crap to you, it gets absorbed on a cellular level, but now I'm like, 'life's too short', just do your own thing anyway.

It might be hard at first, but it's important to just take pockets of time for yourself during the day, even if it's only twenty minutes, to do something just for you that makes you happy, like go to a nice coffee shop, read a newspaper, or a book or magazine. Whatever it is you like doing, just take time out for yourself. See it as time for you to take control over your own life, because you want to take responsibility for what's happening in your life. It's easy to forget we have choices, because we can end up blaming other people, and playing the victim game, but the thing is, you can change your perspective and build a strong mindset that will help you to move forward, and take action everyday towards your goals.

Success doesn't happen overnight, and you can't wait for someone to save you either, like in the movies. You know, the one where it goes, 'When will my prince come? My prince will come and he'll save me, and I'll never have to work a day in my life.' Life doesn't work like that, we all have to go out and make a living and pay the bills.

My vision really feels stronger than ever! I want to establish 'The Body Positivity Collective'. I want to build a team of women who help other women with their business ideas, for example teenagers, graduates, and young women at university who are trying to figure out what they want to do with their life.

I want to help them to start their businesses much earlier, to build their vision and support them in getting their idea off the ground.

You don't have to wait until you're in your mid-thirties to figure out what you want to do with your life.

I want to help women to be the best that they can, to inspire them, and motivate them to do what they want to do with their life because life's too short to regret things.

If you try it and it doesn't work out, at least you tried.

You don't want to spend your whole life wishing you tried and wake up too old to do something.

I want my future kids to be secure and to be able to have the best schooling, to be able to travel as much as they want, and to expose them to different experiences and cultures. To inspire them to value their freedom and to make their own choices. To not feel they ever have to stay stuck in a certain career or lifestyle they don't want for themselves.

I'm all about helping people and giving back to people that need it the most. People can't always afford to do lots of courses and not everyone is lucky enough to go to university, or have parents to support them.

I want to be able to give a scholarship to younger women, who have the potential to develop a business idea, and mentor them through the steps, to gain their confidence, stand in their own power, and help them navigate through what's happened to them in the past so it doesn't hold them back.

It may be hard for a while, trying to find and step into your power. There may be adversity and things you have to overcome. The most important thing is we are alive. We have this amazing life to adventure through, the best part is we can do it together! We can help each other.

The time is now to be positive, to be grateful for what you have because when you're grateful for what you have, the most incredible things will come to you. Just wait and see!

ABOUT THE AUTHOR

Bridget had it all on paper. The high-flying IT job, the gorgeous apartment on the waterfront in the beautiful city of Wellington, New Zealand, the fancy holidays, the gym membership, but something was missing.

It was the need to find inner happiness and joy. Her body was crying out for love. She abused it in all the wrong ways.

Bridget was diagnosed as pre-diabetic and decided that it was time to turn her life around by consciously making healthy decisions and learning to love her body again, not punishing it.

She decided to stop hiding and start shining.

BRIDGET ZYKA

The Body Positivity Coach.

  @thebodypositivitycoach

Shannon Garrison Negi

CHAPTER 12
From Corporate Burnout to In Love With a Beautiful Life
By Shannon Garrison Negi

"I will no longer be the woman who defends her thoughts, opinions, or actions to herself or anyone else."
– Cara Alwill Leyba

There are many defining moments in our life when we have to choose which direction we want our adventure to take. And, the funny thing about change is that it happens when you least expect it (or think you need it).

One of those moments for me, when everything seemed perfect, is exactly when all hell broke loose and I had to decide if I was going to keep banging into a brick wall or lean into the change that my soul was really calling me to do.

Perfection is a myth. Say, what!?

Yes, I had the Baby, the Dog, the hot Husband, the new House (white picket fence and all) and I had just landed my dream job working for a startup in the sports industry here in the US. Sounds perfect right? I thought so too but, let me give you the details, and you can see for yourself why looks can be deceiving.

I was employee number four at my new job, and I thought it was amazing. I was going to help to build a company from the ground up, my way. I guess the entrepreneur in me was trying to peek it's head out even then (early 2015) because I LOVED being able to create things my way, to have a say in how things got done and shape the growth of a company. I always see the good in any situation, and I was ecstatic about this one.

For the first ten months leading up to Super Bowl 50 (any Bronco fans reading this?), we worked hard. We went from zero to forty million with less than ten employees, put on one of the best parties of the year at a huge sporting event and I had the most insane year of operational business growth I've ever had running all of our departments.

Now here's where it got interesting.

After our success, new management was brought in (we had been operating without an official CEO up until this point) and with change, of course, brings uncertainty. After several months, a new office back in midtown Manhattan (commuting sucks), lots of new employees brought onboard and a lack of communication about what direction this company was going, things were not feeling right to me.

Around this same time, an old friend (circa elementary school) had been every so often sending me notes about this company she had joined, and its fabulous products. I was a non-responder until June of 2016 when she sent me yet another sweet note asking me if I wanted to try some suntan lotion and self-tanner!

Now timing is everything no matter what business you're in and it just so happened that the timing for me at the moment I received her note was perfect.

I really didn't know exactly what I was looking for that summer but day in and day out I was dreading going to work, so I knew something had to change. I got on the phone with her to find out about the opportunity. She was passionate, excited and genuinely happy. She also had a full-time job, three kids and a hectic life, which told me that this business could be done around that. I jumped in, figuring that if my family buys products and I make dog food money, it will have been worth it.

Fast forward only two months, and it turns out that what I had been missing all along was a whole network of fabulous women supporting each other through all the things we go through in life and business. I had worked with a lot of men given the industries I was in previously, and my environment always gravitated toward the more masculine energy. I had run into so many women who weren't supportive that I had convinced myself that I didn't get along with other women. The fact is, I just needed the RIGHT women in my life!

It didn't take much longer for me to know that the freedom this opportunity provided was what I wanted for my family's future. I didn't want to feel trapped. I didn't want to keep missing out on my babies' daily lives. After seventeen years of grinding to make my way up the corporate ladder, finally, this was something I could control and the icing on the cake? There was no glass ceiling!

Now having a paycheck while you grow your side hustle is the safest way to do it. I was petrified of not having a steady income and decided to grow this into something that would provide us with the life we craved over the next three years.

Shortly after that, we found out we were pregnant with our second daughter and the day that I was going to tell my new boss the news (assuming of course that I would then have another year or so at this company) they let me go. Umm, yeah, I know exactly what you are thinking, and you should have seen his face when I said I was pregnant! My gut had known it was coming and really it was a blessing in disguise (paid off the IRS & banked some severance). I signed a three-year contract (which kept me right on track for my plan) within a month of working for my old mentor and was excited to get into a new position.

I walked into what was pretty much chaos, and that's the kind of energy I thrived on in a corporate setting. For years I was the fixer, bringing a fresh set of eyes, changes to process and usually a better way of doing things to the different companies I had worked for. My new job was to help a radio station in New York really get clear on where they were going, what they were doing in the future and how they were going to save money doing it. I was exactly where I wanted to be. But, I was also pregnant with my second daughter. This created a dynamic with my boss that did not make it easy for me to show up to work every day. There seemed to be this cloud of judgment if I wasn't sitting at my desk at 8:00 am or working late every day.

Now let me say this, I LOVED my career. I couldn't wait to get back to work after having my first daughter because that was all I knew and I thought that defined me as a successful woman.

The funny thing about having another kid is they shift your perspective A LOT. I had already started thinking to myself, 'How do I do this when I have another baby? How am I going to leave her all day every day?'

Being in a position to help others grow, learn and thrive lights me up. I love the hustle and bustle of getting shit done. I've always been very driven to succeed, however you want to describe the word. For me it was getting promoted, getting that raise, making more money. That is how I had been shown from a young age what it meant to be successful so, in my head, that's what it meant for me. Even if I was unhappy, as long as I made more money and as long as I had more responsibility, then I was successful. So, being in a leadership position at a huge company was success, right? How quickly perspective can change.

About a week before I was to go out on maternity in May of 2017 I was let go, again (ouch). Now it sounds pretty awful, I mean who fires the nine-month pregnant VP of Finance? But in my heart, I knew that the thought of going back after this baby would have been so much worse than this. I took my severance and went home to figure out exactly how I was going to make my side gig work as a full-time deal, which was about two years sooner than scheduled.

Do you see the pattern yet? The Universe always gives you exactly what you need even if you think you aren't ready! I knew that this was the Universe pushing me off the cliff and saying, 'Stop messing around. Stop playing small. Stop trying to fit into a box that you don't fit into'. This was my fifth job that hadn't worked since I left the music business, and I obviously hadn't been listening until now! I definitely got the message this time!

I embraced my full-time entrepreneur role immediately, working from the hospital after I had the baby, during the night when I was up feeding her. I remember thinking about how much freedom I now had to work anywhere. I told my husband, 'This is what we're going to do. We've got severance until October. We're going to make this work.'

That summer was one of the best. I was able to spend a ton of time with my new daughter. I was actually home, present, not worried about going back to work and I cooked a lot (sidenote: I LOVE to cook, and I am good at it!).

Now, this seems like the ideal scenario, but when I look back on it, I didn't spend enough time getting my business in order nor setting myself up for success. In fact, I worked it like it was my corporate job meaning I was working 24/7 (definition of work hard is different for a corporate person). When October rolled around, and I was nowhere near to replacing my income, I started to get nervous. This was the point when I realized I was stuck and needed some help. My business wasn't growing (no wonder if I was working like a maniac, who wants to do that?) and I was going to need income to keep living the life I was accustomed to. What exactly was my long-term goal with this and how the hell was I going to make it happen?

Being financially free and having time-freedom is, I believe, the majority of the world's goal. We all want that; we all want to have more time with our kids, money in the bank and our debts paid off. But, that by itself, is not enough to drive you to work as hard as you need to or to push someone to take the steps necessary to grow a business into something that can support a family of four (and two dogs). The entrepreneur life can be very simple, but it's not easy. I was hovering around $1,000 a month, and that just wasn't going to cut it.

I started looking for more inspiration online as I didn't want to feel like I was doing it on my own – because what I was doing wasn't working. It was a huge step for me to admit that I was going to need support to fix it (anyone else a control freak here?). My husband and I had diversified our side business and in the process met a really amazing social media queen who showed me how to navigate the online space and grow my following. But, I still lacked clarity on exactly what was I doing and who I was serving.

It was around this time that I discovered my first business coach, Lauren Eliz Love. I joined her community, and I eventually booked a discovery call, even though I was petrified. Asking for help had never been my strong suit. I came from an environment where asking for help was a weakness, and you just didn't do it unless it was an emergency. So yes, I was resistant to change, but the alternative was going back to a job I probably wasn't going to like for less money and being away from my kids. Umm, no thanks! That was enough to get me in motion.

I ended up hiring this beautiful person whose energy I couldn't get enough of. It was a twelve-month group program; I was committing to this for myself and my family. This was a group of motivated women, and it was exactly what I needed at that moment.

I think it's important for all of us to remember to trust those good feelings and that little intuitive voice when it's telling you things are right. For so long I did what I thought was the right thing versus what actually made me feel good, so this was a big step forward into this new life I was creating. Imagine that, good things coming when you trust yourself? Ah-mazing!

This is the part of my journey where I went head-over-heels into my feminine energy. I ran as far away from my financial background and the masculine energy I had always embodied as fast as I could (There was no balance here). I dove head-first into essential oils, crystals, you name it – anything that related to the spiritual side of things, I wanted part of it. I know you are all thinking I am crazy at this point, don't worry my husband did as well. He walked into my office one day, and there were crystals everywhere, and he just looked at me and said, 'What the heck is going on?' I needed the time to really get back in tune with myself and understand who I was outside of my career as an accountant and my life as a mom. I'm not sure he understood it, but he left me alone.

'Who am I going to help?' Was the biggest question that kept coming up. I've been a people-pleaser my whole life. I want to help everyone, and I quickly realized that trying to help everyone was not getting me anywhere (my side hustle was the perfect example).

The funny part about that whole period on this journey was that I really didn't believe I was going to go into coaching. I thought my network marketing journey was going to be enough, but as I started to let my 'She Power' out (thanks Cassandra, for that beautiful phrase), I really focused on my self-care by eating properly, doing yoga, meditating, and having a dedicated workspace. My creativity blossomed, and I felt calm and connected to my mission to help more women take control of their life. It took this to see how burned out I really was and that's when I realized if you are not making enough time for yourself, if you're not in a good space of flow, your business isn't going to grow.

But wait, how the heck did you pay for all of this? I know you are all probably wondering where I was getting the money from after my severance ran out. Well, I did something completely taboo, especially for a finance person, I pulled my 401K and never looked back. It probably sounds completely insane to someone, not in this situation, but I just knew with my heart that this was how we survived while I figured out myself and my business.

By spring 2018 I knew I was onto something. I was going to inspire hundreds of thousands of women to live a life they're really proud of living and not just have to go to a nine-to-five every day. It was a huge relief to actually figure out what this mission was. How exactly to go about building this empire I envisioned was next on my to-do list. My business brain was back in action, and I needed a strategy to scale and scale quickly. That's when I met my one-on-one business coach, Jennifer Hardie, who is the queen of tech and has the most vibrant energy of anyone I've ever met. I knew right away that I needed to hire her and we were going to go out there and take over the world (stay tuned, this is still a work in progress)!

The time had come for me to stop running away from my past and embrace that brilliant money side of me that I had been stuffing into a small box and ignoring. There were people out there who needed what I had to offer.

In September 2018, I traveled to Bali with nine other amazing women (and one fantastic photographer) for the week that altered the course of this journey. This was the week where I became ultra-clear on who it is that I serve. I checked my excuses at the door and realized just how freaking fabulous I really am.

Seriously, why did it take me so long to figure this out?

This wild adventure I am on has not been all roses and unicorns; I am continually learning about the ladies I serve and want to serve as well as all the new trends for being an online entrepreneur. It can be exhilarating and exhausting all at the same time.

I couldn't be more excited for what is to come as I step into the next version of myself. I consistently show up to put myself out in the online world, and I know it's working even though it can seem like nobody is watching half the time. I know how scary it can be. A lot of us are in this position where you want to run your business but there are so many moving parts, and you don't actually know if it's going to work. You must keep going.

I am stepping into this future version of me, who is ridiculously successful. Who travels around the world helping other people and inspiring women to go after their dreams, someone who actually spends time and is more patient with her kids while going to all of their events and taking them to school every day. Stepping into the someone I always knew I could be.

It's a big piece of why I wanted to share my story. If I inspire one person to step up and actually own their future, take control of their life and get unstuck from a job or situation that is no longer serving their needs, then my mission is a success.

Now, I've started at the current state of my journey, I am guessing you all want to know some of the beginning now, right?

Let's go back to the early years that brought me to this path. It's funny, I've really struggled with sharing this piece of my life because unlike so many people I see in this space, I do not have some kind of trauma or event that shaped the person I am today (comparisonitis anyone?). I was so concerned what people would think about not having a rag-to-riches story that I've kept it mainly to myself because really it's a riches-to-riches story. I have been very successful in my career up until this point.

The truth is I really wanted to delete this whole section of my chapter when I was editing because I am of the mindset that I do not let my past experiences define how my future is going to go. I learn from it, grow through it and move on to the next thing I want to accomplish. WE all make mistakes, take a wrong turn on this crazy life road but what really matters is how you come through it and what you do with the lesson you learned.

I am sure some of you are thinking, there must be some good stuff in there! So, I will tell you about some of my past, so you know where I've been but always remember that where I am going is so much more important.

I grew up in a middle-class neighbourhood in southern California, we are real California natives. Both of my parents were from Los Angeles and I grew up in the OC (yes as in the show)! I had both sets of grandparents around the majority of my life, and we had a big extended family. Some of my fondest memories are being with my cousins. My dad's family is quite large. There was seven of us that would spend the summers together in northern California. We rode horses and got to be kids. I reminisce on those times now and hope that my kids will actually get to enjoy their time as kids. It drives me every day in my business to keep showing up to give them that life.

My parents were divorced before I was ten so we lived between two households most of the time. We always had a nice house or apartment to live in, nothing extravagant, but my mom made sure that we had enough.

We loved music in our house and grew up going to concerts, air-guitaring to Duran Duran and choreographing dances in our apartment complex to Madonna's first album. Those were the days of carefree kid life.

I got good grades, was involved in school activities (I had played the flute since third grade), had a good group of friends and enjoyed school. I knew if I was smart enough and kept up my grades, I could get into a good college and get a good job so that I hopefully made more money than my parents.

One of the turning points in my young life that had a big impact on future me, was when my dad got remarried the first time and moved away to Colorado. It left me needing attention which drove a lot of my revolt during those teenage years. My mom would say I was the worst teenager, but I call it strong-willed and independent. Even then I always went after the things in life that I wanted. I didn't drink, I didn't do drugs, I just loved life (and meeting boys because sixteen-year-old me of course was all about boys).

I should update here that after several years of not having a great relationship with my dad, we were able to work it out. My dad has since remarried again to an absolutely smart, wonderful lady who gave me a younger step-sister and brother, as well as a crazy, extended family that I adore.

Now, going off to college was an entirely different world. That crazy teenager that I had been was allowed so much freedom! I went to USC which wasn't my first choice of school, but I went anyway because they gave me a scholarship. I was having the time of my life and almost got kicked out of school twice in my first two years. NO parents, no curfew, no attendance taken at class meant I got to go a little crazy. I hung out with football players, went to clubs, went to work and did everything I wanted when I wanted to do it.

I look back, and I think how that was all part of this journey as well. If I hadn't gone through some of those things, changed schools, made a choice to go to community college for a year then transferred to LMU where I met some people that I am still friends with to this day, then I would be on a totally different journey.

It took me two extra years to finish college. I'm pretty sure my parents thought I wasn't going to graduate at all, ever. But, I did, finally, with a Bachelor's Degree in Science.

I had a job in accounting waiting for me and was finally getting my life in order. It really was just a mindset shift. Doing homework and working almost full-time was getting to be a cramp on my lifestyle, so it was time to finish up and get the next phase of life moving.

Now aside from being a wild child in college, I did always have a job. I had to work to have money to pay for food and going out if I was going to have fun. My parents helped with school, but we weren't rich in the terms most of us think. I had great jobs throughout this time, met wonderful people, had flexibility, and learned a lot about business and life.

When I look back on it now, it's crazy. I was flunking out of school, in debt and decided I was going to be successful anyway. Just a reminder that you always have a choice which way your life is going to go.

One of the things I learned from my parents is that we work hard and we do our job well. Most of my ideas about money came from watching both of my parents work very hard for their money all of my life. My mom had an interior design business for as long as I can remember, so the entrepreneur example was present daily for me as I was growing up. My dad was in sales and network marketing as well, so I had been exposed to the freedom life from a young age (and yet it still took me twenty years to choose that path).

What I knew from watching them was that I could do anything I wanted, but I was going to have to work really hard to make money and create my life. Why do we always think money has to be hard to make?

So, I started climbing the corporate ladder. Even then I knew the power of relationships and went out there to make the best ones I could get. I made my way through the ranks in public accounting. I got promoted year after year, received the best training, traveled, counted Grammy ballots and got to do a ton of things that I think a lot of people don't ever think about doing. My life was pretty fabulous.

Five years into my career is a big promotion for most people in public accounting, and there was one manager who stood against me, so I knew it was time to go do something else (another mindset shift). I took a job I was petrified of, packed up my stuff and moved to Boston. I left behind the life that I knew and loved because I had to take a chance on myself.

One of my passions in life is traveling. I love being on a plane, exploring new places and when I got the chance to travel for work, I took it. This job allowed me to travel all over the world helping companies buy other companies, it was incredible. I was truly living a fabulous life (on an expense account of course).

I definitely didn't feel like the smartest person in the room anymore. For anyone who has dealt with imposter syndrome, I had it bad at this time in my life. I was surrounded by incredibly smart, talented people who had chosen me to be on their team, why did I want to sabotage myself? This kept a cloud over my office life in Boston, I just never felt as if I could be me (outspoken, passionate, a bit wild). Looking back on this now, I realize that I was suppressing the real me, trying to fit into a life that just wasn't necessarily where my soul belonged. (It sounds so woo woo, I know!).

One thing I knew about myself even back then was that I was good at my job, I was passionate and tended to speak my mind. I knew I was a badass, but at this time in my life I hated to brag about myself or 'show off'. I was seen as controlling, loud and overbearing, something that plagued me throughout my corporate career wherever I went. I know I am not the only one who has struggled with this, right?

Why did we ever think it was ok to dim our light to be accepted in certain places?

But back to the year I spent in Boston that ended in what I always call the week that changed my life. This was one of the pivotal moments in my young life.

SO...leading up to that week a lot happened. Let me start with my sister since she was really the catalyst for this change.

When I first put this story together, I realized I had inadvertently not mentioned my sister until my late twenties. I think that says a lot about how not close we were when we were younger versus when we grew up. She and I were only two years apart, but she was the younger sister who always bugged me (sorry Kimmy), and during her sophomore year in high school, we both moved to Colorado, I wrecked my dad's car and ended up coming back right when school was starting, but she stayed. So, when she returned to California after a year, and I was on my way to college, we didn't have much in common at the time.

Fast forward to before I made the move to Boston, we had started hanging out more. I think we were just more grown up. We had both gone through experiences in our younger years and our college years, and as we started to grow a little and become better people, it was time to be friends again.

I haven't spent much time talking about my passion for music, but let's just say it's a huge part of who I am. When my sister and I started hanging out, she had become an aspiring musician. She was managing a club in San Francisco, and due to my work travel, I ended up being around quite a bit. One weekend I met a band she always booked who were from Southern Cali, the World Wide Spies. My life would never be the same.

The year I turned thirty (I was still living in Boston), I went to South by Southwest with this crazy group of band guys to help them play the festival. Some of you from the States may know what SXSW is, but for those who don't, it's a huge week-long music festival. We drove from LA to Austin, Texas towing a trailer. This was the week that changed my life. I was not Shannon the accountant that week, I was Shannon, the passionate music manager who could talk her way into any show and was surrounded by creative, amazing people.

When I went back to regular life that next week, I knew that a massive change had to happen. I saw the years flash before my eyes, and I knew with every ounce of my being that this was not the life that I wanted to lead two years from now, let alone five or ten years down the road. I saw the way everyone else was going, working twenty-four hours a day, always traveling, what kind of life was that going to be?

So, what did I love? I loved music. I always have. It was time to embrace that love and do something with it.

Two and a half months later I was laid off and went to NYC to look for a job (my sister wanted to move there so why not?). The very last interview of a long week was with a man I am lucky enough to have had as a mentor for many years since that first meeting. I got the job, but I had to move back to Los Angeles as the position was in Burbank. Sometimes you have to go with the flow; nothing had felt so right for me until this point.

Now I was using my skills as a CPA and immersed in an industry I was super passionate about. I made connections, traveled the world and was back to living my dream life.

Turning thirty was the start of the best five years of my life. I was doing all of the things I wanted; I was young, single and did the things that made me crazy happy and kept me passionate even when I was working my butt off for others.

What's the thing that lights you up? Have you spent time doing it? If you are reading this and you haven't done it, this is your permission slip to get out there.

I could go on for many more pages about all of the crazy things I did in those five years, after I truly let my passion take over. I started that job in music the week after July 4th, 2006 with a suitcase full of jeans and hoodies and never looked back.

My sister ended up moving to LA with me. We rented a fabulous penthouse on Wilshire Blvd, went to every show our friends played in and around LA, and I worked hard. I also met one of my best friends at this time. We became partners in crime, traveling around the world together to see bands, helping our friends on the road and living our most amazing life.

I wanted nothing more than to help all of these amazing people I was meeting in bands around town also live their dream lives.

I still loved accounting, it was my bread and butter, but now I loved teaching people how it could help them in their own businesses.

One of the biggest takeaways from this time in my life was being able to live my passion daily, spending time doing things that I loved and not dimming my light for anyone.

Even back then some people didn't understand how or why I was living this fabulous life. People thought because I was very close to our boss who ran the show at the music company that I was getting special treatment. People wanted to know why my life was so fabulous and theirs wasn't? It was a choice to only do things that I loved and enjoyed. But, one thing people didn't always realize is that I worked extremely hard for what I had and did. I bordered on being a workaholic at this stage in life. I wanted people to know that I did my job well even if I was taking conference calls from South Africa, or by the pool in Argentina while I saw Duran Duran (ask me about that story sometime).

That's when I knew the laptop life was for me and I took full advantage of that in my career. I also came to a conclusion at this point that for me sitting at a desk all day was not going to be the end of my life. There was no way I was ever going to be happy sitting in one place all day, every day. The wanderlust had gotten me, and now my dreams were even bigger than before.

In 2009 I moved to New York City where I have spent the last nine years of my life, and a lot has changed in that time (all for good, don't worry).

I met my husband in 2010 while working together at the music company. He's in IT. I didn't know his name, I just knew he was the 'hot' guy. We actually dated for a year before people even knew that we were dating. I am not sure either of us thought it was going to turn into the long-term relationship we have now. We just went with the flow. I always knew I wanted kids but there was absolutely no urgency to do that, and I didn't even know if he was the one I wanted kids with yet!

Now, all good things, sometimes, must come to an end. In 2011 I was laid off from that job in music and it was not something I was prepared for. Like I said before, change comes when you least expect it.

The next few years after that really were tumultuous, to say the least. I went through several jobs – advertising, back to music, indie movie distribution, and then the sports company I already told you about, but nothing seemed to be the right fit. I didn't realize that it was the Universe trying to push me out of this box I had put myself in. I just kept looking for the next thing that would make me happy to show up every day, and surrounding myself with people who didn't understand my life.

Finally, in 2014 my husband and I decided to get married. It was a crazy year! We are people that like to do stuff when we want to do it, so that first year we did all the things they tell you not to do! We bought a house, got a dog, had a baby, and changed jobs. I laugh because here we are almost nine years later, with two kids, two dogs, and another new house in a different state. It's been quite the wild ride.

He's always been my biggest supporter and pushed me to take a chance on myself last year. He may still ask me when we will be making millions, but he loves seeing me happy and fulfilled in my new role.

WE both know that living a life of freedom is ultimately where we see ourselves, and being able to give our babies the choice to also do what they want in life is the driving force behind everything we do.

For the record, both my kids have their own frequent flyer numbers and are already living the digital nomad life with me, even if they don't understand what it means. It's so fun being able to show them the world.

One thing I've noticed, as I've documented this part of my life, is that I have control issues. It's taken me almost twenty years to understand that if you let go, if you just release control of what's happening, and go with it, everything always works out. Seriously, why couldn't I have learned that in my twenties!

It may not always feel like things are going to work out, when you are in the middle of it. Every time I've lost my job, I was never fully prepared and spent a ton of time blaming myself wondering where I went wrong, and how I could have done something different. But these things have led me on a journey to find my passion again, and for that, I'm forever grateful.

I also used to be a complete people-pleaser. I wanted everyone to like me, and it took me a really long time to be okay with not to being everyone's cup of tea. The best thing I did for myself lately was stopping giving a f*ck what anyone thinks of me. This is my life, and other people's opinions don't pay my bills.

It's my job to take care of myself and my family and to make sure that I'm happy.

Another big lesson that came out of all the things I went through in my corporate days, is that you really have no control over other people. People are going to do what they want, and you just have to understand that it isn't about you, it's about them. Make sure that you're happy with your actions because that's the only thing you can control. I am always operating as the highest version of myself. I do what inspires me with courage and passion. I love what I do, and that makes showing up every day that much easier.

Life lessons are learned when you need them and not before. It's all part of the journey. If I didn't have all these great things that happened to me as well as some of the bad stuff, I wouldn't be the person I am today. Who knows what my life would have looked like? I took a chance on myself long ago and then another chance, and there will be more chances because I'm betting on myself to create this life. We only get to live it once and I am determined to make this my best.

It seems that everyone I talk to lately is waiting for something to happen, or waiting for the perfect moment. I'm just going to share a secret with you! There is no perfect moment.

If you don't take control of what you want your life to look like, six months from now, a year from now, five years from now, you're going to look back and say, 'What the heck happened and why didn't I do any of the things I wanted to do?'

I've always been one to live my life the way I wanted, and so many people thought I was absolutely nuts. People are afraid to take chances, which makes me incredibly sad for them.

Something else you should know? Listen to yourself. Listen to that voice that's telling you if something's wrong. It's telling you if something's right. We are taught to ignore the inner voice, to play it safe and how has that worked out for you? If I'd started listening to that sooner, who knows where I would have been.

Go with the flow. Listen to your intuition more. And do what makes you happy.

What makes you happy? If it's having a glass of wine on your porch, then do it. If it's going to the movies, do it. Whatever it is, do the things that make you happy because that's really what life's all about. Not the busy work and not the stuff everyone else tells you to do either (unless it vibes with you).

I live to be inspiring, but if I'm not happy and living my best life, how the hell can I inspire others?

In Bali, this past September, a Shaman told me I had amazing, spiritual energy and that I was going to help a lot of people. I cried after this moment. I knew then, without a shadow of a doubt, that I had been playing small and holding back from showing up in the world as the most powerful version of me.

So remember, you always have a choice. You don't like where you are at right now, stand up and do something about it. Change your circumstances, start that business, go on a trip, drink the expensive bottle of wine, whatever it is that you've been putting off.

Remember who you are, the version of yourself that isn't afraid to shine brightly.

It's ok to be selfish in the pursuit of the things you love in life. You are responsible for your own happiness.

Surround yourself with people who lift you up, pick you up when you are down and want to see you win no matter what's in it for them.

I promise that you are absolutely deserving of all of the things you have been dreaming about.

It's time to Embrace the Brilliance that already exists within.

With so much love,
Shannon x

ABOUT THE AUTHOR

Shannon is a former corporate finance executive turned multi-passionate entrepreneur who recently relocated from NYC to the suburbs of Colorado with her 2 gorgeous daughters, husband and giant fur babies.

She's a business strategy coach who specializes in money, confidence & creating visibility online for the ridiculously busy mom who's ready to make herself a priority.

For years she's been providing financial and strategic decision support to companies around the world including Deloitte, Warner Music, Kaplan Thaler, Capitol Records, NFL On Location Experiences and iHeartMedia. From saving $500k in expenses to growing a company from $0 to $40m in its first year, her experiences have given her the knowledge she needs to help others get free on their terms.

She's driven by her heart to help other moms strategize to make their dreams a reality and she's in the process of scaling her business into a global platform to be able to help as many people as she can.

She believes that everyone should understand how to make money with ease and design a life they are in love with.

Fun facts about Shannon – she makes the best bowl of popcorn you may ever have, she's a wine snob & she cannot live without mascara or lip gloss.

SHANNON GARRISON NEGI

Business Strategist, Money Expert, Confidence Booster, Social Influencer & Crazy Mom.
www.shannongarrisonnegi.com

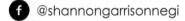 @shannongarrisonnegi

 @embracingthebria (group)

@shannon_t

Jennifer Hardie

ABOUT THE CURATOR
Jennifer Hardie

As a serial entrepreneur, abundance hacker and within a year, multi-6-figure business owner, Jennifer is on a mission to serve 1 million women, around the globe, who are ready to step into their best selves.

As a mother of 3, she understands the pressures of motherhood whilst building an empire and wants to ensure that women realise that you can absolutely have it all! It's a case of working smarter not necessarily harder. Realising her passion for making women feel on top of the world she put together an online Digital Marketing Programme helping women understand the tech and strategies behind growing their businesses to 6 figures and beyond. Her heart absolutely lies within coaching, empowering other women to step into their greatness and realise their true potential.

In addition to programmes and courses she also has a successful podcast and tv show on YouTube, holds business retreats and VIP days around the globe and this collaborative book writing project for female leaders and influencers to share their story.

Jen has been featured on STV, BBC TV & Radio, Thrive Global and Huffington Post to name a few. She is the Scottish Ambassador for Ladies of All Nations and has many philanthropic projects on the go.

Her heart absolutely lies within coaching, empowering other women to step into their greatness and realise their true potential.

She believes it is time we stand up to celebrate the rise of the Renaissance Woman!

JENNIFER HARDIE

Award Winning Business Coach, Digital Marketing Strategist, Speaker, Writer, Author & Philanthropist.
www.jenniferhardie.com

Unstoppable TV: **www.bit.ly/jenniferhardie_youtube**
The Unstoppable Podcast Show:
www.bit.ly/UnstoppablePodcastShow

f @jenniferhardie.me

f @jenhardieunstoppable (business)

@jen.hardie

in @jenniferhardieunstoppable

@jenhardie100

@jenniferhardie1000

"Whilst people may only read about this world, be the person who dances on into it."

– Jennifer Hardie

A LOVE LETTER

Dear Self,

From now on, I promise to look after you as if you were made from porcelain and precious stones.

This is a non-negotiable.

I'm going to look at what I have created as my reality...

The relationships that have flourished and those that have ended. The work I am producing in the world. The people I serve. The creative outlets. The exhilarating highs, the almighty lows. The joys. The struggles.

I'm going to reflect on the times that I was at my most aligned and happiest, then work with precision and vigour on, not replicating, but producing an environment in which that alignment and happiness can thrive.

My heart is happy, my body is healthy, and my soul is fulfilled, creative and on fire for life.

Today I will reflect on my journey.

Today I will admire myself.

Today I will take pride in how far I have come.

I understand that I have been gifted with my perfect imperfections for a reason and that the mission I have been set relies on each of those qualities, the perfect and imperfect in equal measures. My uniqueness shall now be given the spotlight and I will embrace each part of my being with open arms.

In this moment I will revel in awe at all that I've endured to step into my higher self and purpose!

I am powerful.

I am protected.

I am supported.

I am free.

I am completely unstoppable.

With all my heart and adoration,

Love always,
Me x

> "Why is everyone trying so hard to be happy, why can't they
> just be happy now?"
> – Ruby Hardie, Age 7

INVITATION

Dear amazing reader & friend,

We have come to the end of this time together!

I have a sense that you may have felt a connection to our authors, resonate maybe or even see a little of your journey in theirs?

I hope from the bottom of my heart that you enjoyed reading this as much as we have all enjoyed writing it for you!

I actually hate endings, don't you?!

And because I do, I felt it necessary to give us a way to stay together for longer!

The Unstoppable team, authors and I wish to invite you into our online community...

'The She is Unstoppable™ - Secret Society'

You can find it by searching via Facebook or by typing the link below into you search engine...

www.facebook.com/groups/sheisunstoppable.secretsociety

In this page we shall be offering free motivation, words of wisdom, solving problems and coaching when desired.

We shall be sharing open-minded conversations surrounding some incredible heart-warming subjects as well as the controversial, hard-hitting topics that we feel too afraid to share our opinions on!

Being a part of this community means that you are forward-thinking with a desire to make or be a change for good in this often-crazy world.

This is a place for nurture, care, love, support, patience, understanding and compassion!

Let's begin to make this world a little happier and better off than we found it. After all, on our own we are a drop, but together we are an ocean... WE ARE UNSTOPPABLE!

It would also be incredible if you came over and followed us to be kept up-to-date with all that we are creating at She Is Unstoppable™. Here are the links...

 @she_is_unstoppable_book

 @sheisunstoppablebook

We cannot wait to welcome you into the family and get to know you!

See you in there!

Lots of love,
Jen, Our Incredible Authors & Team Unstoppable x

"If the only prayer you ever say is thank you, that will be enough."

– Eckhart Tolle

CPSIA information can be obtained
at www.ICGtesting.com
Printed in the USA
LVHW080520290619
622764LV00009B/252/P